HERE IS OUR GOD

Here Is Our God

GOD'S REVELATION OF HIMSELF IN SCRIPTURE

KATHLEEN B. NIELSON AND
D. A. CARSON,
EDITORS

CROSSWAY

WHEATON, ILLINOIS

Trade paperback ISBN: 978-1-4335-3967-1
epub ISBN: 978-1-4335-3970-1
PDF ISBN: 978-1-4335-3968-8
Mobipocket ISBN: 978-1-4335-3969-5

Library of Congress Cataloging-in-Publication Data
Here is our God : God's revelation of Himself in scripture /
Kathleen B. Nielson and D. A. Carson, editors.
     pages cm
Includes bibliographical references and index.
ISBN 978-1-4335-3967-1
  1. God—Biblical teaching. 2. Bible—Criticism, interpretation, etc.
I. Nielson, Kathleen Buswell, editor of compilation.
BS544.H45   2014
231.7'4—dc23   2013048894

Crossway is a publishing ministry of Good News Publishers.

VP		24	23	22	21	20	19	18	17	16	15	14
15	14	13	12	11	10	9	8	7	6	5	4	3	2	1

Contents

Preface

Why not leave The Gospel Coalition 2012 National Women's Conference in Orlando and on TGC's website? Why stretch its life into a book?

We suggest four reasons—the first without a doubt being the *focus of the biblical teaching* that occurred in the eight plenary sessions collected in this volume. The talks trace a series of great "theophany" passages throughout the Scriptures, passages where God displays himself in spectacular revelation. The overall goal for these talks was to gain from God's Word a renewed vision of God and his sweeping purposes of redemption, as he shows himself to us through his revelation. We left the 2012 conference knowing we had paused and seen God more clearly together in his Word. We had gloried in God's redemption, through Jesus Christ. Through this volume, by God's grace, the conference's theme will keep calling: "Here Is Our God!"

The second reason for this collection relates to the *mix of the biblical teaching*: three men and five women. Such a mix at a TGC women's conference reveals all kinds of commitments. It reveals a common commitment on the part of these eight expositors to the clear, expositional teaching of God's inspired Word. It reveals the commitment of TGC's pastor-leaders to value and encourage the women of the church in studying and teaching the Scriptures. It reveals the commitment of the women participants to value and embrace the leadership of such men. It reveals one joyful glimpse of men and women working together in the Word and for the gospel—not focusing specifically on men's and women's roles but just working together within the context of shared commitments about those roles. These collected talks offer a harmony of distinct and unique voices, a harmony we delight to share. As you read, we hope you will picture the context of a women's conference, with several thousand women gathered and listening with energy.

The third reason to compile and share these talks is to offer encouragement through the *context of the biblical teaching*. How crucial for the church to be raising up strong women of the Word—women who know it, love it, declare it, and live it. What that means, of course, is that we want to be raising up women who shine forth Jesus, the one who shines from the Bible's pages from beginning to end. We want the church to be full of women whose lips and lives declare: "Here Is Our God!" Not every woman is called to be a teacher in the formal sense, like those who taught at the conference. But we all teach. Women are teaching others all the time in all kinds of ways. We need an increasing number of godly models who can encourage women to handle and communicate God's Word with clarity and humble strength in all the contexts of our lives. The 2012 conference was full of the live encouragement of women to this end. May this book extend that encouragement into many far corners of the church.

We said repeatedly that the 2012 conference was for

women but not all about women. The conference was about our God who reveals himself in his Word and redeems his people through his Son. The final and most important point, then, is the *goal of this biblical teaching*: to exalt the Lord God of the Scriptures. That is what we hope for this collection of talks and for the reflection/discussion questions that follow each one. As we take in the Word, by the Spirit, may God be glorified.

Kathleen B. Nielson,
Director of Women's Initiatives, TGC

D. A. Carson,
President, TGC

1

On the Mountain

THE TERRIFYING AND BECKONING GOD

Exodus 19

TIM KELLER

Since I was the first plenary speaker, I should say something about the gathering itself. We gathered to connect women who hear and do Bible exposition. TGC did not bring women together to talk and think about women but to talk and think about God. Every culture of the world by God's common grace has its peculiar glories and tends to be attentive to and aware of things in Scripture that at least some of the other cultures don't see. They bring their various exegetical riches and theological understanding of the infallible Word of God to the whole church, and that enriches the whole church. That must also be true of both genders. For women to come together to hear and do Bible exposition certainly enriches all of those gathered, and it will enrich the whole church.

We're considering together the theme "Here Is Our God," looking into passages where God reveals himself in spectacular ways to his people. Exodus 19 is a great place to start. It's an important chapter, so important that several key New Testament texts refer directly to it (e.g., Hebrews 12 and 1 Peter 2). In Exodus 19, Moses and Israel come to Mount Sinai to receive the Ten Commandments. Chapter 19 does not contain the Ten Commandments, but it sets them up. The passage divides into three basic sections:

1) The History and Order of Grace (19:1–8)
2) The Terrifying and Beckoning God (19:9–19)
3) The Going Down of Moses (19:20–25)

1) THE HISTORY AND ORDER OF GRACE (EX. 19:1–8)

The History of Grace

The first couple of verses tell us something about the history of grace. Alec Motyer makes a good observation concerning these first two verses.[1] You wouldn't think of this unless you were a biblical scholar who keeps a map in his head as he is reading. He says that God and Moses basically told the Israelites, "Trust us. We're going to take you to the Promised Land, to a land flowing with milk and honey, to Palestine." And the children of Israel trusted them. But Sinai is farther away from the Promised Land than Egypt. Sinai is actually south. So God led them almost in the opposite direction from where he said he was going to lead them. They were supposed to go

---

[1] J. Alec Motyer, *The Message of Exodus: The Days of Our Pilgrimage*, The Bible Speaks Today (Downers Grove: InterVarsity, 2005), 190–92. This is a tremendous book. You couldn't do any better at understanding the book of Exodus, which is a long and very complicated book.

to a land flowing with milk and honey, yet God took them to a desert, a mountainous desert (v. 2). The land was far worse than Egypt. And that's where God met them.

It is often so: you give your life to Jesus and say, "I'm putting everything into your hands. I'm trusting you with my whole life." And then you watch things go downhill from there. Weeks later, months later, a couple of years later, you ask, "What happened? I gave myself to him. I trusted him. And everything is getting worse and worse." If you admit it, you are farther away from the things you had hoped God would give you. You think, "I gave God everything. Surely he'd give me this and this and this. You know, if he wants to." God seems to be taking you in an opposite direction. So often the history of grace in our lives follows this pattern: God seems to be taking us away from where he said he is going to take us. My two favorite penultimate examples of this pattern both happened at Dothan.

Example 1. The book of Genesis records that Jacob had twelve sons. Because he loved his wife Rachel more than his other wife, Leah, Jacob favored Rachel's sons over all the others. That utterly poisoned everything and everybody in that family. This was a case of overt parental favoritism. It poisoned the life of Joseph, who was one of Rachel's two sons. All the pieces were in place for Joseph to become spoiled and arrogant even though he was only a teenager. He could have been on his way to being an absolutely cruel, awful person. Their whole family system was broken, suffering the effects of selfishness and sin. The other brothers were bitter and cynical: they had a love-hate relationship with their father, and they were angry at Joseph and Benjamin. It was a mess. One day, in the area of Dothan, far away from home, the brothers who were out shepherding saw Joseph come to them. They threw him in a pit and sold him into slavery in Egypt. And there it was, you might say, that Joseph turned to the God of his father: in the pit, on the trip, and in the dungeon where he ended up in Egypt and pled, "Get me out of here!"

Silence. Many years of silence.

Example 2. Something happened in Dothan years later. The prophet Elisha and his servant were locked up in the besieged city of Dothan (2 Kings 6). Elisha's servant panicked, thinking that they were going to lose their lives. Elisha prayed. Then the eyes of Elisha's servant were opened, and they both could see chariots of fire all around the city. God delivered Elisha and his servant dramatically from this besieged city.

That's the way it's supposed to be!

One guy prayed and prayed and nothing happened for years and years. God never seemed to answer his prayers. Another guy prayed and saw chariots of fire.

Now, when we get to the end of the book of Genesis and the end of Joseph's story, we see that God's grace was as operative in Joseph's life as it was in Elisha's life. But here's the difference: Elisha's immediate need was a fairly simple kind of salvation. He needed help from an army. But Joseph and Jacob and all those guys needed something way deeper. They needed their souls saved.

What if God had just showed up to Joseph early on and said something like this: "You are a spoiled brat. Do you realize that if you keep going the way you are, as self-centered as you are, you're going to destroy your life, and nobody's going to like you? You're going to make a mess of your marriage."

Have you ever tried to do that with a teenager? He won't listen to you.

John Newton, the great hymn writer, wrote in a letter, "Nobody ever learned they were a sinner by being told. They have to be shown." It took years for God to break open Joseph and his brothers and his father to grace. At the end of Genesis, Joseph says, "You intended to harm me, but God intended it for good to accomplish what is now being done, the saving of many lives" (50:20).[2]

Joseph's descendants, who grew into a great people, got to the Promised Land through the desert. They were looking for the Promised Land, but God took them to the desert. In the desert he would meet them. The desert was the way to the Promised Land.

The ultimate example of this pattern is Jesus. He shows up and preaches the kingdom of God. Think of his followers responding, "Yes! The kingdom of God! Lion lying down with the lamb! Every tear wiped away! Yeah!" The next thing you know, Jesus is on the cross, dying in agony. Imagine some of Jesus's followers looking up at him and thinking, "I don't know what good God could bring out of this." We know, of course, that the way to get to the resurrection is through the cross. The way to get to the ultimate resurrection (the new heavens and the new earth) is through the cross, through Jesus's going through that desert, loneliness, and suffering. If Jesus wants to come back and end evil and put everything right without ending us, then he had to go to the cross. Again, the way to the Promised Land is through the desert.

---

[2] Unless otherwise indicated, Scripture quotations in this chapter are taken from *The Holy Bible, New International Version®*, NIV®. Copyright © 1973, 1978, 1984 by Biblica, Inc.™ Used by permission. All rights reserved worldwide.

So often that is how grace works. Are you ready for that? John Newton said, "Everything is needful that he sends. Nothing can be needful that he withholds." Think about that for the rest of your life. It'll do you good.

The Order of Grace

Alec Motyer sees three things in Exodus 19:4–6.[3] The sequence of these central elements is extremely important for understanding the whole Bible:

1) The saving acts of the Lord (v. 4)
2) Our response of obedience (v. 5a)
3) The blessing that the obedience brings (vv. 5b–6)

Motyer says that nothing must ever be allowed to upset this order: (1) salvation by grace, (2) obedience, (3) blessing. Nothing in your mind must ever upset that sequence. That's the order.

To put it another way, God did not appear and give the children of Israel the law and then have them promise, "We will do everything the Lord says," and then reply, "Good. I'll save you. I'll take you out of Egypt on eagles' wings." No, God just saves them.

Do you know what it means to be carried on eagles' wings (v. 4)? Israel didn't fight their way out of Egypt. They didn't even run out or walk out in this sense (of course, they literally did). What God is trying to get across is that when an eagle carries you, you don't do anything. You are lifted up and moved from one place to another. It's sheer grace. It has nothing at all to do with your performance.

So God saves you by sheer grace and then says, "Because I

---

[3] Motyer, *Exodus*, 196.

saved you by sheer grace, obey me." He does not say, "Obey me, and I'll save you." No, it's, "I've saved you; now obey me."

Motyer adds that the whole narrative from the Passover to the exodus to Mount Sinai is "a huge visual aid before our eyes."[4] It's a visual aid. Of what? Of the gospel!

An Israelite could have said this:

> I was in bondage under penalty of death. I was a slave in a foreign land. But I took shelter under the blood of the lamb. And I was led out and saved by the mighty arm of God. I did nothing at all to accomplish it. The Lord did it all for us his people. He saved us by his sheer grace. Then we came to the place where God showed us how to begin to live out our salvation. He gave us the law. And now we haven't reached the Promised Land yet, and we often fail and fall; we certainly aren't perfect. But we even have a way of constantly dealing with our sins through the atoning sacrifice, through the blood. And we'll eventually get to the Promised Land.

That's what an Israelite could have said during this period of time. And a Christian can say every one of those things, too.

Alec Motyer is absolutely right. This story is the most astounding visual aid. It's the gospel writ large. You'll never understand the whole Bible unless you understand the order: (1) grace, (2) obedience, (3) blessing. It's not (1) grace, (2) blessing, (3) obedience. Nor is it (1) obedience, (2) grace, (3) blessing.

If it was law then deliverance, we would say, "You obey; therefore God accepts you." But since it's deliverance (the exodus) and then law (the Ten Commandments at Mount Sinai),

---

[4] Alec Motyer, *Look to the Rock: An Old Testament Background to Our Understanding of Christ* (Grand Rapids, MI: Kregel, 2004), 39–40.

the gospel is this: "God accepts you; therefore, you obey." A Christian says, "I'm accepted because of the blood of Jesus Christ; therefore, I obey." There is nothing more important to understand.

Superficially, a person who operates under "I obey; therefore, God accepts me," and a person who operates under "God accepts me; therefore, I obey" are probably both trying to obey the Ten Commandments. On the surface they are both trying to obey. But the person who understands the gospel, who understands this sequence, will be motivated by love, joy, and gratitude. The other person is operating out of fear. It is self-centered to say, "If I obey, then God will bless me and answer my prayers and take me to heaven." Why does such a person obey God? To get things. But a person who already has everything in Jesus obeys not to get things from God but to *get God*, to please, resemble, love, delight in, and honor him. Those are utterly different inner dynamics.

The obedience of a person who says, "I'd better obey so that God will deliver me" is always conditional. This person thinks, "I'm really pretty good. I've been doing everything I should. I've been praying and reading my Bible. I've been exercising sexual self-control. I've been charitable to the poor. And my life isn't going very well. But *she's* not doing any of those things, and *her* life *is* going very well. What's going on?!" If you ever feel like that, then you've probably got the sequence wrong. You might get an A in your Exodus exam, but you don't get what the story of Exodus means. If it's true that you obey because you've already been accepted, then what would the conditions be? You're saying, "I'm doing this because of what I've already received from him."

God says, "I saved you. Now obey me, and then these blessings will come." And God names blessings (vv. 5b–6). God doesn't say, "I want to make my covenant with you." He says, "I want you to keep my covenant." The hint is that God is saying, "I've already brought you into a relationship with me. Now I want to make it formal." In other words, the blessings are there for you; they are yours in principle because God has saved you by his grace; but it's through obedience that you'll actually realize them.

What are those blessings?

1) "You will be my treasured possession."
2) "You will be for me a kingdom of priests."
3) "You will be for me . . . a holy nation."

1) "You will be my treasured possession." "Treasured possession" refers to the personal wealth of an ancient king. In those days kings were absolute monarchs, which meant that they essentially owned everything. If you were the king of a land, practically speaking you owned everything in the land. But this word refers to one's private, personal wealth or possessions, something that you love so much that you put it in your room as your own personal delight. On the one hand, God already treasured Israel, or he wouldn't have saved them. On the other hand, God says, "If you obey me fully and keep my covenant, then out of all nations you will be my treasured possession." That's why Motyer is right in saying that God is already treating Israel as a treasured possession, as a jewel. Yet God is saying, "I want you to obey into that kind of relationship. I want you to obey so that we can treasure each other." Think of how obedience works in a relationship like that.

If you fall in love with someone, you try to find out what pleases that person, what delights that person, what that person likes. Then you want to surprise that person by giving it or doing it. You might not think of it this way or use this term, but you are seeking the will of the beloved when you do that. You are trying to find out your beloved's will, what your beloved wants. And you are complying. You are essentially obeying your beloved's will. Why? Because you want to delight your beloved.

Some years ago in some lectures on legalism and antinomianism Sinclair Ferguson explained the gospel this way: "God accepts you; therefore, you obey." Legalism is, "You obey; therefore, God accepts you." Antinomianism is, "You really don't have to obey. Either there is no God, or God accepts you no matter how you live. He loves and accepts everybody."[5] Sinclair argued that most of us tend to think of legalism and antinomianism as opposites, but they are actually the same: they both oppose the gospel because neither understands the grace of obedience. Most antinomians are ex-legalists who are broken under the fact that they could never understand *why* we must obey, that is, to treasure our treasure, to be treasured by our treasure. It's a love relationship.

But that's not all.

2) "You will be for me a kingdom of priests." A priest has access to God, but, in particular, priests are mediators. They bring people together. Priests bring people who are outside into a connection with God on the inside. If we have a relationship of love in which we are God's treasured possession,

---

[5] Sinclair B. Ferguson, "The Marrow Controversy," sermon (2004), http://www.sermonaudio.com/gpts.

not only will others see and desire that love, but also we will be able as God's people to bring other people in, to show them the way to come into relationship with the God who made them. We get to be a whole kingdom of priests.

But that's not all.

3) "You will be for me . . . a holy nation." A *holy nation* literally means "a different kind of human society." *Holy* means "separate, distinct." God is saying, "I want you to obey so that you really will be different."

The gospel shuts up your ego and gets it all sorted out so that you're not constantly whiplashing between (a) thinking too much of yourself and (b) being down on yourself. The gospel does this by (a) humbling your ego into the dust with knowledge that you're a sinner and (b) affirming it to the sky by telling you rightly that you're now a son or daughter of the king and that you can't lose that status. As C. S. Lewis taught, you don't think less of yourself or more of yourself; you just think of yourself less. What beautiful community you can have then. What remarkable, transparent relationships. What comfort. How wonderful. No pecking order. No biting and devouring each other.

"Holy nation" doesn't just refer to good relationships. It also implies that money, sex, and power operate completely differently when the ego is sorted, and therefore a godly human society with changed hearts will be a community that shows the world something amazing. Jesus, the light of the world, says to his disciples, "You are the light of the world." That describes what a holy nation is. The Sermon on the Mount describes a holy nation. If we really lived like that, if we really lived as God's treasured possession, as a kingdom of priests, as a holy nation, we would be the light of the world.

So why do you obey now, as a believer? Not to get accepted. Not to get out of Egypt. You're already out of Egypt. You obey to know, love, serve, and display Jesus. Everything about this differs from the Canaanite religions of the time. For example, most of the ancient cities were built around a ziggurat, a kind of pyramid that served as a temple. The temples were built like that because the priests and holy people would go up to the top to find their god, to offer sacrifices, and to get the favor of the gods. What do you think Mount Sinai is? It is God's chosen ziggurat. It's a pyramid. We don't build ourselves a ladder and go up to find God. We don't say, "We're going to do this and offer sacrifices so that God must bless us." All other religions say, "If you do this and this and this, then you will reach God." Christianity says, "In Jesus Christ, God came to find you." God comes down. You don't go up. God descends.

"The Lord said to Moses, 'Behold, I am coming to you in a thick cloud.' . . . Now Mount Sinai was wrapped in smoke because the Lord had descended on it in fire. . . . The Lord came down on Mount Sinai, to the top of the mountain" (vv. 9, 18, 20 esv). God comes down.

Even the commands about washing and having no sex (vv. 10–15) are a way of saying, "We will not be like the Canaanites, like all the other religions. Our religion isn't just a little bit different. The very way we approach God is exactly the opposite in every way." Only the God of the Bible comes down.

This is all because of his grace. "I carried you on eagles' wings and brought you to myself," God says (v. 4). That's grace.

Mine heart owns none before thee,
For thy rich grace I thirst;
This knowing, if I love thee,
Thou must have loved me first.[6]

2) THE TERRIFYING AND BECKONING GOD (EX. 19:9–19)

God is simultaneously frightening and approachable. The visual and auditory effects are astonishing:

> You have not come to a mountain that can be touched and that is burning with fire; to darkness, gloom and storm; to a trumpet blast or to such a voice speaking words that those who heard it begged that no further word be spoken to them, because they could not bear what was commanded: "If even an animal touches the mountain, it must be stoned to death." The sight was so terrifying that Moses said, "I am trembling with fear." (Heb. 12:18–21)

That passage in Hebrews 12 mentions seven things:

1) Fire
2) Deep darkness
3) Gloom
4) Storm
5) Trumpet blast
6) A voice
7) You'll be killed if you touch the mountain. God says, "I might break out against you. You might perish, so don't get too close."

---

[6]Josiah Conder, "'Tis Not That I Did Choose Thee," 1836.

God is not a warm fuzzy. Maybe somewhere else it's different. Let's see:

- God appears to Jacob as a terrible wrestler.
- God appears to Job as a hurricane.
- God appears to Moses as a blazing fire (twice).
- God appears to Joshua as a man of war armed to the teeth.
- God appears to Ezekiel. Just look at Ezekiel 1. I don't know what he saw, but it was overwhelming. He saw the glory of God. It's one of the most astonishing things written in any kind of human literature. Ezekiel was trying to describe it, and he just sort of went nuts. And some pretty good commentators make a pretty good case that Ezekiel was trying to describe something that words just can't describe.
- God appears to Moses again in Exodus 33. Moses says, "Show me your glory." And God says, "I can't. It would kill you."

Why? What is so terrifying about God?[7] Why are the people trembling? Are they afraid of getting hit by lightning? No, it's much more profound than that. The terrifying nature of God does not have to have visual and auditory accompaniments at all. Why the terror?

We are in such deep denial about how bad we are. If we could actually see what sniveling cowards we really are, what depths of cruelty we are really capable of, I think we would die. Even the most experienced and mature Christians to a great degree rest their self-regard and ability to look in the mirror and look others in the eye on their being pretty good people. They still have a self-image based largely on their

---

[7] I won't go into too much detail here because John Piper will be dealing with Isaiah 6, the greatest passage in the Bible explaining what it means to encounter the holiness of God.

virtue. Every culture has a different way of expressing this, but most people tend to think, "I'm a good guy, a decent person; I work hard." But if you actually saw what you're really like, you would die. It would be a self-quake. You would just disintegrate.

I once talked to a counselor at an Ivy League school who said that most of the people who get into the Ivy League haven't had a B+ since pre-kindergarten. To a great degree, their self-image is based on the idea that they are smart, that they're the smartest kids in town. That's how they look at themselves in the mirror and look other people in the eye. It's a disaster to get into an Ivy League school, because everyone else is just as smart, and the professors can't give everybody As. These professors are under enormous pressure to give everybody As because the kids can't take it emotionally to receive anything lower. But somebody's got to get a B and a C. The students are experiencing a self-quake: they thought they were smart their whole life, but now they're surrounded by people who are clearly smarter than they are. They can't keep up. It's incredibly traumatic. They end up on the couch in the counselor's office, saying, "I don't know who I am!" If getting into the presence of human superlatives practically decimates you, what must it be to be in the presence of God? Even a sense of the greatness of God makes you feel tiny. Even a sense of the holiness of God makes you feel impure and flawed. Even a sense of the beauty of God makes you feel absolutely shriveled and ugly. That's why Isaiah, when he got near God, said, "I am unclean." That's why Peter, when he got a vision of Jesus's greatness, said, "Depart from me, O Lord, for I am a sinful man." You just fall apart.

You don't have to have thunder and lightning. Recently I was preaching through the Sermon on the Mount and found something very interesting. Virginia Stem Owens, a professor of English and literature, was teaching a university course some years ago at a major secular university.[8] She gave her students the exercise of reading the Sermon on the Mount and writing a response paper to it. Some of the students hadn't heard of it, and very few had any acquaintance with it at all. When she read the response papers, she wasn't surprised, and yet she was. They hated it. They utterly hated it. In the context of nineteenth-century liberal theology, people used to say, "The important thing is not what you believe about doctrine. It's that you just live according to the Sermon on the Mount because it's just so beautiful. That's how a Christian ought to live." But they clearly had never read it. When these students read it, they said things like this:

- "I did not like the essay 'Sermon [on] the Mount.' It was hard to read and made me feel like I had to be perfect and no one is."
- "The things asked in this sermon are absurd. To look at a woman is adultery? That is the most extreme, stupid, unhuman statement that I have ever heard."

Virginia Stem Owens knew that the students were desperately looking for cover, because when you read the Sermon on the Mount, you know that this is how you want people around you to live. You just don't think that you can do it yourself. You realize, "This is an arrow pointing at my heart." Virginia Stem Owens's conclusion is that, finally, biblical illit-

---

[8] Virginia Stem Owens, "God and Man at Texas A&M," *Reformed Journal* 37, no. 11 (1987): 3–4.

eracy has come to the point where people are able to respond to Jesus without filtering it through two thousand years of "cultural haze." Now, "the Bible remains offensive to honest, ignorant ears, just as it was in the first century."[9] When we hear the Bible as it is, it's terrifying.

I think it was Dr. Lloyd-Jones who said, "If anyone has ever read the Sermon on the Mount with an open mind, they would fall down and cry out, 'God, save me from the Sermon on the Mount.'" Because what they are experiencing in a little way without the thunder and lightning and special effects is the holiness of God.

C. S. Lewis puts it remarkably:

> An "impersonal God"—well and good. A subjective God of beauty, truth and goodness, inside our own heads—better still. A formless life-force surging through us, a vast power which we can tap—best of all. But God Himself, alive, pulling at the other end of the cord, perhaps approaching at an infinite speed, the hunter, king, husband—that is quite another matter. There comes a moment when the children who have been playing at burglars hush suddenly: was that a *real* footstep in the hall? There comes a moment when people who have been dabbling in religion ("Man's search for God!") suddenly draw back. Supposing we really found Him? We never meant it to come to *that*! Worse still, supposing He had found us![10]

If there is a God, you are, in a sense, alone with Him. You cannot put Him off with speculations about your next-door neighbors or memories of what you have read in

9 Ibid., 4.
10 C. S. Lewis, *Miracles* (1947; repr. New York: HarperCollins, 1996), 150.

books. What will all that chatter and hearsay count (will you even be able to remember it?) when the anesthetic fog that we call "nature" or "the real world" fades away and the Presence in which you have always stood becomes palpable, immediate, and unavoidable?[11]

Now there's an evangelistic pitch, the best one I've ever heard.

Yet God does not come only in fire but in a cloud: "I am going to come to you in a dense cloud" (Ex. 19:9). God is actually impossible to bear, yet what is he doing in a cloud? Alec Motyer answers, "[He is] so shrouding (not abandoning or diminishing) his glory that he could accommodate himself to live among his people, to grace them with a presence which, in its awful holiness, would spell their destruction."[12] Even there he is showing, "I still want you in my life, and I want to be in your life. And I know we have a problem: a sinner cannot live in the presence of a holy God. I want you still."

How can this terrifying God be a beckoning God? Or, to put it another way, how can this God of both fire and cloud (which means a God of both absolute holiness and yet love) be satisfied? He wants holiness and justice and truth, yet he wants us in his arms. How is that going to happen? The answer is a mediator.

3) THE GOING DOWN OF MOSES (EX. 19:20–25)

What's going on? We're not totally sure. Motyer and other commentators think that the people were getting lax. They got near; it was scary; yet God would not have brought Moses up simply to say, "The people are in danger of trying to come

---

[11] C. S. Lewis, *Mere Christianity* (1952; repr. New York: HarperCollins, 2001), 217.
[12] Motyer, *Exodus*, 207.

up to get me." The point is: "Moses, be a mediator. Go down and warn them and keep them from dying."

Moses was the mediator. Moses was the man on the mountain. Moses was somehow going to be able to keep the people from perishing. He was the go-between. He went down.

In Hebrews 12 we have an answer as to why it was possible for God even to come to the people in a cloud back then and why we are in a very different situation now:

> You have not come to a mountain that can be touched and that is burning with fire; to darkness, gloom and storm; to a trumpet blast or to such a voice speaking words that those who heard it begged that no further word be spoken to them, because they could not bear what was commanded: "If even an animal touches the mountain, it must be stoned to death." The sight was so terrifying that Moses said, "I am trembling with fear." But you have come to Mount Zion, to the city of the living God, the heavenly Jerusalem. You have come to thousands upon thousands of angels in joyful assembly, to the church of the firstborn, whose names are written in heaven. You have come to God, the Judge of all, to the spirits of the righteous made perfect, to Jesus the mediator of a new covenant, and to the sprinkled blood that speaks a better word than the blood of Abel. (vv. 18–24)

When Cain killed Abel, it was the first murder, the first act of overt human injustice. Abel didn't deserve to die. Cain murdered him:

> The LORD said, "What have you done? Listen! Your brother's blood cries out to me from the ground." (Gen. 4:10)

And there are other places where the Bible talks about injustice like this. Blood spilt cries out, "Justice! Avenge me!"

The author of Hebrews has the audacity to say Moses was a mediator who kept the people in some kind of relationship with God; he kept them from being killed by God. But Jesus Christ was the *ultimate* mediator. Why? Because when he died on the cross, his blood cried out, "Grace! Accept them! Yes, they have sinned, but accept them because I have paid their penalty!"

What happened to Jesus on the cross?

> From noon until three in the afternoon darkness came over all the land. About three in the afternoon Jesus cried out in a loud voice, *"Eli, Eli, lema sabachthani?"* (which means "My God, my God, why have you forsaken me?"). . . . And when Jesus had cried out again in a loud voice, he gave up his spirit. At that moment the curtain of the temple was torn in two from top to bottom. The earth shook, the rocks split. (Matt. 27:45–46, 50–51)

The temple curtain was like the cloud. It kept the people from being killed by the shekinah glory. But what happened is that Jesus was shaken. The darkness came down on Jesus; the judgment of God came down on Jesus; the thunder and lightning came down on Jesus. So now we don't need the cloud (or the curtain), because right into our lives comes the holiness of God. Jesus who knew no sin became sin for us, bore God's wrath for us, so that in him we might become the righteousness of God (2 Cor. 5:21). We become holy. We can approach the mountain. We *are* the temple now.

What does that mean? On the one hand, it means absolute

joy. We can understand this idea of being God's treasured possession in a way that the Old Testament saints could never have understood. We have absolutely no excuse for not having an intimate prayer life with the God who has revealed himself to us and not only kept us from perishing but also allowed us to be forgiven and to live in loving intimacy with him—with no cloud or curtain in between.

But on the other hand, we still need to be holy. Look what he has done for us!

Because he was shaken (according to the book of Hebrews), we can live unshakable lives.

CONCLUSION

The rest of the New Testament is just playing out what we have read here in the Old Testament. Dr. Lloyd-Jones often said that he loved the Old Testament because it conveyed pictorially, narratively, and vividly what the New Testament often expresses propositionally. So here is the gospel. We have a holy God who wants his people to see him and who makes a way for them to do that without perishing. The Old Testament is full of clouds and mediators by whom people are delivered from the fire of God's holy presence. This God is fire, but this God is also merciful. The God of Mount Sinai is also the God who carries his people out of bondage on eagles' wings. By his grace he saves us, and then he leads us (through the desert) to the Promised Land. But we don't have to wait until the Promised Land to enjoy the fruit of his salvation. Even in the desert he meets us and has fellowship with us. He calls us to live as his people, loved and treasured by him. So Exodus 19 lets us meet this God, but it is not until we come to the New

Testament and to the cross that we can truly come right up the mountain alive, safely into his holy presence, and look into the face of Christ, the final, perfect mediator.

From beginning to end the Bible calls out, "Here is your God!" We'll hear this call through all the passages expounded in this book. The call in Exodus 19 is an important one at the start. It shows us the history and the order of God's grace. It shows us both a terrifying and a beckoning God. And it shows us through the story of Moses how this God provides a mediator for his people, wanting them not to perish but to live—to live forever as his treasured, holy possession. This is our God.

REFLECTION AND DISCUSSION QUESTIONS

1) God shows himself to his people in Exodus 19. Sum up what the people see and what God is revealing about himself.

2) List all the evidences of God's grace and mercy you find in Exodus 19.

3) What is God after, in Exodus 19? What verses reveal his purpose(s) at work?

4) Tim Keller helps us connect Exodus 19 to the New Testament and to the Lord Jesus Christ. How would you put that connection in your own words? What New Testament passages connect most helpfully?

5) What will you take away from Exodus 19? Consider questions like: How might taking in this revelation of God affect your thinking and living? What kinds of prayers might Exodus 19 lead you to pray for yourself or for others?

2

In the Temple

THE GLORIOUS AND FORGIVING GOD

1 Kings 8

PAIGE BROWN

To Moses and then through Moses, God introduced himself to his people as "I AM"—the name that represents his eternal, self-existing, sovereign reality—the truth of who he actually is (Ex. 3:13–15). For this covenant-making God, "I AM" promises "I'm In." I will be your God. You will be my people. I'm *in*. And immediately, as is the case when anyone promises us he is "in," we want to know: *How* "in" is he? That big question is progressively answered throughout the Scriptures with the temple. First Kings 8 is the platform passage from which we will grab onto the structural cable of the temple and ride it like a zip line as we do an all-too-brief aerial study of the I AM God who lovingly became I'm *in*.

First Kings 8 contains the temple dedication scene. This

temple, which Solomon built, is so important that three chapters of the Bible (1 Kings 5–7) are given to its construction. It is a permanent, twice-as-big, grander, splendid-er, gorgeous-er version of the tabernacle. It was built with costly stones, covered with cedar sent from King Hiram of Tyre, overlaid with gold, with intricate carvings everywhere, and furnished with costly vessels. The preceding chapters show us its glittering grandeur, its limitless value and worth. Solomon has already built a palace for himself, a palace for a king, but this is *the* palace of *the* King.

So, how *in* is he?

1) THE INHABITANT GOD *IN* A BUILDING

Occupation

Solomon had delayed this dedication for eleven months so that it could be part of the celebration of the Feast of Tabernacles. This was the pilgrimage feast commemorating the wanderings of the people of Israel, wanderings that had long ago ended for them in permanent dwellings where the Lord had given them rest. And now God comes to his permanent dwelling to rest among his people. This gorgeous new temple is complete, and King Solomon gathers the people that they may open up the doors and signal to the Lord, "Come in!" And God *really* does.

A little boy asked his Sunday school teacher as he was playing, "Where is God?" And she said, "Well, you know the answer. God is everywhere." He responded, "So is he in the Play-Doh can?" And she said, "Well, yes." And he slapped the lid on and exclaimed, "Well, then, I got him!"

The temple is not a Play-Doh can. God's visible occupation is not an aspect of his omnipresence. This is not his every-whereness. This coming in is his absolutely unique, only-here, like-nowhere-else, personal presence—the personal presence that is manifested in the cloud. Though the cloud is not new to Israel (it had led them through the wilderness), this is a new home. And even in this dazzling structure, the presence far outshines the premises. The glory of the Lord strikes more awe than the glory of the temple. And God is still holding back. As Professor Ralph Davis says, "The cloud reveals and conceals."[1] It is so strikingly visible that of course it means he's *there*. Yet it veils the full blaze of his glory because they could not have survived it. They can see it, but they can't see him—so the cloud is both the showing and the covering of his glory. There is still a hiddenness and a mystery. But even cloaked in a cloud, when he comes *in*, they are rightly chased *out*. The cloud is temporarily expulsive to be instructive. It does not change who he is to them; it reminds them of who he is to them.

My favorite book is *To Kill a Mockingbird*. Though it covers the antics of the children trying to bring out Boo Radley, and it covers the unjust trial of Tom Robinson in the pre–civil rights South, Harper Lee's novel is not about those things; it's a story about a little girl's relationship with her father. The climax of this story comes right after the gut-wrenching guilty verdict at Tom Robinson's trial. In those days, the evils of segregation demanded that African Americans sit sequestered in what was called the "Negro balcony" in the courtroom,

---

[1] Dale Ralph Davis, *The Wisdom and the Folly: An Exposition of the Book of First Kings* (Ross-shire, UK: Christian Focus, 2002), 81.

which is where the children—Jem and Dill and Scout—had spent the many hours of the trial with their legs dangling over the banister. The guilty verdict has just been handed down. Atticus has run over to try to console Tom, when they both know that there is nothing that can be done. He then turns wearily to put his papers in his briefcase and begins to walk out the center aisle.

"Miss Jean Louise?"

I looked around. They were all standing. All around us, and on the balcony on the opposite wall, the Negroes were getting to their feet. Reverend Sykes's voice was as distant as Judge Taylor's:

"Miss Jean Louise, stand up. Your father's passin'."[2]

Atticus was already her father. And she already loved him a lot. But she needed to be reminded of who he was.

The cloud comes in, and God's people don't merely stand up. They are chased out. They need to be reminded. That's the effect of his coming in.

But look at the catalyst of God's coming in. The shekinah (Hebrew for "dwelling") glory does not come in with the gold. The shekinah glory doesn't come in with the furnishings. The shekinah glory doesn't come in with the king. The shekinah glory doesn't come in with the priest. The shekinah glory comes in with the *ark*. First Kings 8:21 describes the temple as a structure to house the ark of the covenant, which is mentioned eight times in the first few verses.

The ark of the covenant ushers in not just the glory of a

---

[2] Harper Lee, *To Kill a Mockingbird* (New York: HarperCollins, 1960), 241–42.

cloud but the glory of God's covenant relationship with his people. That covenant relationship is the uniqueness, the like-nowhere-elseness. The glory of Israel, the purpose of Israel, is *that* relationship. In the midst of God's omniscience, he is in effect saying to Israel, "Though I know everything, only you have I known." And in the midst of his omnipresence he is saying, "Though I am everywhere, only here do I dwell. And I'm not coming in without this box. I'm coming in with this box."

So the response provoked by this passage is not, "What's in the cloud?" but "What's in the ark?" Verse 9 tells us: it contains the literally handwritten transcript of his will for us—the Ten Commandments, the code of the covenant relationship. God's glory comes in and takes a seat right there on top of that box, right there on top of those tablets. That is the reason he comes in with the ark but not with the prayer. He comes in with his word, not because of their words. Note the order of the passage. Solomon's prayer does not cause God's coming in. God's coming in causes Solomon's prayer. And yet how could they respond to his coming in? How could they respond to God's loving summons, when they can't keep the commandments that are in the ark? They can respond because those tablets are covered with the mercy seat. They have a cover. They are not exposed. We cannot meet God at the ark. We have to meet him at the altar. That's where God and man must meet. So he provides a mercy seat, a covering for the contents of the ark.

But that covering requires a big, yucky mess right in the middle of this gorgeous gold building. Can anything be as strange as all this gold and all this blood, all at the same time, all in the same place? In 1 Kings 8, we have the pinnacle scene of the entire Old Testament. This is the high point of the history of Israel, here in this simultaneous setting of indescribable splendor and incalculable gore. This is where God comes in. Really *in*. One could ask, "Where is God?" And you could point and say, "He's in that building." That's where he lives. That's where he has chosen to be. He is *that* in. Now that he is there, they move forward with dedication.

Dedication

This is nothing like our building dedications. It's not boring, for one thing. There is no list of people to stand and thank, followed by polite clapping, finger sandwiches, and punch. This is not a public acknowledgment of hard work or unity or sacrifice. This is nothing but a celebration of the fulfilled promises of God. The covenant promises of God are the foundation of this temple. The promises of God have brought his occupying glory to this temple. Solomon declares that "there is no God like you," who keeps what he declares—and then three verses later begs God to keep what he declares (vv. 23, 26). You've kept your promises, so keep your promises. This dedication is a day of leaning more fully into the promises of God in ever greater expectancy. The people know what he has done. And yet Solomon pauses also to say not only that they know what God has done; they know who he is. They know his mystery, that he dwells in impenetrable darkness (v. 12); and they know his majesty, that he cannot be contained by heaven and the highest heaven (v. 27).

Then Solomon makes the transition from proclamation to petition with one of the richest words in the Bible, in 1 Kings

8:28. Do you see it? It is the word "Yet." Mark that word. Solomon is bold to use that grammar of grace that separates biblical faith from all other religions of the world. Other faiths are based on "therefore" systems, "so that" systems, in which what follows flows logically from what has preceded. You work hard to give God or the gods a good record, something that will please them or at least appease them, so that he or they have to bless you: I _____; therefore God _____. That's the equation. It's always a causative relationship.

The gospel is never "so that." The gospel is never "therefore." It is always "and yet." It is always "but." There is no causative connection at all. Read the Scripture looking for this grammar:

> Moses: "It was not because you were more in number than any other people that the LORD set his love on you and chose you, for you were the fewest of all peoples, *but* it is because the LORD loves you." (Deut. 7:7–8)

> David: "If you, O LORD, should mark iniquities,
> O Lord, who could stand?
> *But* with you there is forgiveness." (Ps. 130:3–4)

> Jonah: "I am driven away
> from your sight;
> *yet* I shall again look
> upon your holy temple." (Jonah 2:4)

> Jesus: "I have not come to call the righteous *but* sinners to repentance." (Luke 5:32)

> The Prodigal: "Father, I have sinned against heaven and before you. I am no longer worthy to be called your son."

But the father said to his servants, "Bring quickly the best robe, and put it on him, and put a ring on his hand, and shoes on his feet. . . . Let us eat and celebrate. For this my son was dead, and is alive again; he was lost, and is found." (Luke 15:21–24)

Paul: "By works of the law no human being will be justified in his sight, since through the law comes knowledge of sin. *But* now the righteousness of God has been manifested apart from the law." (Rom. 3:20–21)

Paul: "For the wages of sin is death, *but* the free gift of God is eternal life in Christ Jesus our Lord." (Rom. 6:23)

We could continue indefinitely. It is the grammar of grace. It's not causative; it is always contradictory. This is what's true about me, *but*, Lord, save me anyway! Never *because of.* Always *in spite of.* Not *therefore.* Always *but.*

Solomon knows this, and so he proceeds with that grammar of grace, from making statements about what is true to begging for what does not have to be true. From stating that which is inescapable, God's glory, to asking for that which is inexplicable, *forgiveness.* He has been going on and on about the otherness and the greatness of God, and *yet,* he says, hear and forgive. All your promises—all your blessing—all our history—all our future—hinge on forgiveness. Think of the things that Solomon could have asked for in the visible presence of God, and yet he prays at long length about the one primary need: forgiveness.

When Ken Tada asked Joni Eareckson for their first date, he worked out all week to get ready for it. He had to. He knew he would have to lift her again and again throughout the evening. He would have to be able to pull her in that wheelchair all the way up the stairs at the restaurant he had chosen. There was no other way for a quadriplegic. The glaring primary need had to be met in order to move to the primary purpose, which was relationship. The purpose of their date was not lifting. But it was required. The purpose of God's covenant with us is not forgiveness. But it is required. There is no way around it for sinners. It is required in order to move on to his purpose, which is relationship.

Most shocking in this scene—more than the gold-covered building or the animal carnage or even the presence of the glory of God—is the audacity of Solomon's prayer. In the first place, it is audacious in its extensiveness, its breadth. In 1 Kings 8:31–53 Solomon lays out seven petitions for situations that need God's forgiving deliverance, largely drawn from covenant curses forewarned in Deuteronomy 8. Solomon covers the national and corporate sins that bring banishment and exile and drought and famine. And then he covers the personal sins of one man against his neighbor. He is begging for forgiveness in the biggest yuck and in the smallest secret yuck. Read the language again and look for these words: *whenever, wherever, whatever*. The intention is to generalize about the need for forgiveness for everyone, all the time, everywhere. We know there will be consequences, Lord, but please not condemnation. Please forgive. Audaciously extensive prayer.

It's also audacious in its intensiveness, in its depth. Solomon is in effect saying, "We know you live in a high and lofty place. We know that heaven cannot contain you. We know your transcendence. We know that every time we pray you will always *hear in heaven*." (That's the repeated language of every petition.) "But come here to do something about it. Please don't flip a cosmic switch. Come here. Come near. Night and day. Come here to forgive us, to restore us to yourself." And then he goes on to ask, "Be here with your eyes. Be here with your ears. Be here with your hands. Be here with your mighty arm. Be here with all of your senses, Lord."

After spending an afternoon at the National Zoo, the kids and I were eating at a nearby restaurant. We suddenly heard the roar of dozens of motorcycles and looked up to see uniformed officers stopping all traffic in every direction. "Guys, here comes the president. Let's go see him!" We ran out to grab the prime corner spot on the sidewalk as the massive motorcade zoomed toward us. My five-year-old son kept trying to step out into the street. As I was grabbing the back of his shirt, I kept telling him, "Buddy, back up. You can see him perfectly from right here." "But, Mommy, I want to make sure that he sees me!"

The temple is not so much a place for God's people to see. It is a place for them to *be seen*. Glory requires forgiveness, but not so that the glory can be seen. It can be seen by the forgiven and the unforgiven. It is so that the glory may see—that we may actually be seen by him. Solomon is acknowledging the breadth and the depth of their sin as he is begging for this breadth and this depth, this extensiveness and intensiveness of God's forgiving attention to them.

Third, the prayer is audacious in its exclusiveness. Solomon can be so audacious because, as he says in verse 53, we're your favorite! That's what he's saying. "Lord, I'm bold to ask big because we're your favorite; we're your heritage." There is a well-known mock political convention that happens every election year at Washington and Lee University. Several years ago the Mississippi delegation wore this T-shirt: "Mississippi: Last in Literacy, First in Pulitzer Prizes." Crazy but true. That could be Israel's T-shirt: "Israel: Last in Importance, Last in Loyalty, Last in Obedience, First in the Heart of God." Solomon is saying, "I can ask this because you've already said that you love us the best. You love us like you love nobody else." It's audacious in its exclusiveness.

Yet the prayer is also audacious in its inclusiveness. Solomon understands that though God has called ethnic Israel to be a special people, it is not so that they can have a permanently unique status. It's so that they can model a unique status to which he would eventually call all people: "Lord, be here. We understand that we are your mission station. We understand that we have the singular privilege of being the conduit of your redeeming love to the world." One of the petitions is for the foreigner who will be drawn to the Lord's glory in his temple and who will call to him there. The temple was not supposed to be a barrier. It was supposed to be a bridge, that all people may come to the Lord. Solomon asks for God to show himself off in his people, "that all the peoples of the earth may know that the LORD is God; there is no other" (v. 60).

It is a beautiful, bold prayer. But even with humility and confession, you cannot just ask for forgiveness. It's got to be paid for. So they don't throw rice or shoot fireworks or let balloons go at this dedication; they make the blood flow. This ceremony starts and ends at the altar. *That* is why God can see them. He looks through the lens of atoning blood—blood that is daily offered at this temple and annually brought all the way to the mercy seat. The King has not merely invited the prayers of his people; he has instituted a way of atonement. That is the reason he can be this *in* with a people who are admittedly this sinful. Hence the passage emphasizes the magnitude of the blood: 22,000 oxen, 120,000 sheep, "so many sheep and oxen that they could not be counted or numbered" (v. 5). But you know what? God can count them. And it is not enough.

This seems like such overkill, but it is underkill, because the blood of even unthinkable thousands of animals can never pay for sin. But it wasn't supposed to pay for it. It was supposed to point to it. The bulk of these chapters is about the preparations for a great temple. The details are so important only because the temple itself was a great preparation. It was a great preparation for the greater glory that was coming in the fullness and the finality of atonement and forgiveness. The temple was meant to increase their longing, not their independence. And if only that were the story that follows! But within the reign of Solomon himself, Israel begins that downward spiral from dedication of the temple to desecration of the temple.

Desecration

In the very next chapter, 1 Kings 9, God comes back to Solomon to remind him of the conditions of his *in*-ness. "My eyes and my heart will be there for all time" (v. 3). But *your* heart, God continues, and the hearts of those who reign after you, better be here as well! Even so, Solomon is the one who begins the national slide to disaster. The temple as *the* test of the hearts of God's people is central to the books of Kings. Each king's reign is summarized by whether he allowed worship and sacrifice any place else. That is the verdict on every single king, whether he honored God in his temple.

The messes that Solomon outlines in his long prayer, these seven case studies, all basically occur in the books of 1 and 2 Kings. Yet almost none of the kings ever look to God in his temple to forgive and deliver. Instead they plunder his temple for gold and silver to pay off the invaders. The repeated accounts, almost to the point of monotony, are of corrupt worship outside the temple and abominations within the temple. They completely lost sight of God's glory, and therefore, of course, they completely lost sight of their need for forgiveness. In this beautiful scene in 1 Kings 8, the glory of God eclipses the temple. Yet quickly and then perpetually, the temple eclipsed God. It became a symbol of their status rather than a sanctioned site for confession of sin. The temple no longer served as the megaphone of a humble plea, "Come in." It served as a manipulation tool to demand, "Come hither."

God's people treated the temple as a guarantee of God's favor and help, an "ace in the hole," even when the Babylonians were upon them and it was game over. They thought they were indestructible. And we think, "How silly." But what are our manipulations? That possession or that status that makes me think I am guaranteed God's favor, regardless of my relationship with him. Perhaps it's our last name. Of course God loves me; I'm so-and-so so-and-so. Perhaps it's our spiritual heritage or our church membership. Of course God loves me; I've been in this church—my family's been in this church—for generations. This is our pew. Of course God loves me; I have this leadership position. I've written books.

I lead Bible studies. I give away 30 percent of my money. I'm Reformed! Of course God loves me; I'm a plenary speaker at The Gospel Coalition. God has to love me—I've got the thing that guarantees it. And that is exactly what Israel thought. So God tells Jeremiah:

> Stand in the gate of the Lord's house, and proclaim. . . . Thus says the Lord of hosts . . . Amend your ways and your deeds, and I will let you dwell in this place. Do not trust in these deceptive words: "This is the temple of the Lord, the temple of the Lord, the temple of the Lord." . . . You trust in deceptive words to no avail. Will you steal, murder, commit adultery, swear falsely, make offerings to Baal, and go after other gods . . . and then come and stand before me in this house, which is called by my name, and say, "We are delivered!"—only to go on doing all these abominations? (Jer. 7:2–10)

Could he be any clearer? And they hear, but they will not listen.

I was reading to my three-year-old when we heard my one-year-old crying over the monitor. As I got up to interrupt our book, he said, "No, no, Mommy, I'll take care of her." And I thought, "Ah! I have lived to hear those words!" You know what he did? He got up, and he turned off the monitor. Israel turned off the monitor. They hear Jeremiah's words and instead of responding, "What is wrong with us? What have we done?" they just turn off Jeremiah. They put him in a pit—lock him away so that they don't have to hear it anymore.

We have the recorded visions that God gave to Ezekiel of the abominations in the temple: seventy elders of Israel worshiping loathsome beasts and creeping things; twenty-five priests standing at the door of the temple with their backs to it while worshiping the sun. In Ezekiel 8, God says he will close his eyes to them. He will close his ears to them (Ezek. 8:18). And then in Ezekiel 10, the glory of the Lord mounts his chariot of cherubim and he *leaves*. The inhabitant God is the *evacuating* God. How *in* is he? He's out! And the temple is a tear-down.

Yet even as he is leaving, God is making promises over his shoulder. Not lesser promises. Bigger promises. Through the same prophets. "The days are coming, declares the Lord, when I will make a new covenant with the house of Israel and the house of Judah. . . . I will put my law within them, and I will write it on their hearts. And I will be their God, and they shall be my people. . . . They shall all know me" (Jer. 31:31, 33–34). "I will remove the heart of stone from their flesh and give them a heart of flesh, that they may walk in my statutes and keep my rules and obey them. And they shall be my people, and I will be their God" (Ezek. 11:19–20).

There's a school motto that says, "Beyond the Best there is a Better." That's what God is saying: beyond what you thought was the best, there is a better. I am actually coming farther *in*. That is his determination, not because of what is in their hearts but because of what is in his heart. This "better" does not refer to Zerubbabel's rebuilt temple. That was necessary, but it was a lesser, a holding place that made them lean forward saying, "Is this it? Isn't there more? Isn't there something greater?" And God endorses their leaning in Haggai 2, telling them there is a greater glory coming: "The latter glory of this house shall be greater than the former" (v. 9). That greater glory is not Herod's temple, though it was a magnificent structure fitting that king's ego and ambitions. No, God is talking about a greater temple glory in a greater presence.

Could the promises be true? After hundreds of years of silence, would he really come back in? Farther in? More fully in? Oh yes! Now he *really* comes in—in a way no one could have ever dreamed. No longer the inhabitant God in a building, but now the incarnate God *in* a body.

2) THE INCARNATE GOD *IN* A BODY

He doesn't come in now with a chariot of cherubim. He comes in amniotic fluid. When is the next time in the Bible after 1 Kings 8 that we actually see *the* glory of the Lord? Do you remember?

> And there were in the same country shepherds abiding in the field, keeping watch over their flock by night. And, lo, the angel of the Lord came upon them, and the glory of the Lord shone round about them: and they were sore afraid. And the angel said unto them, Fear not: for, behold, I bring you good tidings of great joy, which shall be to all people. For unto you is born this day in the city of David a Savior, which is Christ the Lord. (Luke 2:8–11 KJV)

Is it too familiar to be the craziest thing you've ever heard? The glory of the Lord appears to lowly workers on the night shift as his herald announces, "Do not be chased out. Do not run away. Do not be afraid! He does not come with judgment or covenant curses. Unto you he has come *in*!" *How* in? He is *in* Bethlehem *in* a baby's body wrapped *in* rags lying *in* a barn *in* a feeding trough. He is so *in* that this lowly little scene is the zenith display of his glory in the Scripture. Nowhere else except in visions do we see the host of heaven. Nowhere else do we hear them sing, "Glory!"

Revelation

The temple had been such a strange combination of splendor and blood so that God and man could meet there. Here is the unimaginable combination: the temple in a person, fully God and fully man. He is that same temple God of glory, but now not hidden away in the Most Holy Place for the special high priesthood but revealed in the flesh to shepherds and tax collectors and lepers and prostitutes. John 1:14 says he "became flesh and dwelt among us," and what have we seen? "We have seen his glory." In the flesh. He is the same temple God of glory.

He is the same temple God of forgiveness. Call his name Jesus, for he will save his people from their sins. Unto you is born this day a *Savior* who is Christ the Lord. At his baptism he was revealed to be both the Messiah King and the Suffering Servant in one person. The old covenant provoked true astonishment: Why was he willing to be somewhere? But now there is absolute shock: Why is he willing to be some*one*? One could ask, "Where is God?" And you could point and say, "He's crying in a manger . . . working in a carpenter's shop . . . sleeping on a boat . . . reclining at that table . . . walking through the grain fields . . . teaching on the hillside . . . in Simon's house . . . in Matthew's house . . . in Martha's house . . . in the Decapolis . . . in Capernaum . . . in Bethany." He is *that* in.

Solomon had asked God to be present in the temple with his figurative senses. And now God has come with actual eyes. And he sees Zacchaeus in the tree. He sees the widow of Nain following that coffin. He sees the man by the pool at Bethesda. He has come with actual ears. He hears the lepers calling to him from a distance. He hears Bartemaeus shouting his name. He has come with actual fingers. He touches the eyes of the man born blind. He holds the infants in his arms. He takes Jairus's daughter by the hand and lifts her up. In the temple building God's glory had evicted. In the temple body he has come to embrace. He is a revelation, a reality so astounding that his own apostles cannot grasp it during his life among them. So their query is a refrain in almost every episode in the Gospels: Who is this? Who is this? Who is this? He's the temple.

N. T. Wright says, "The temple has for too long been the forgotten factor in New Testament Christology," because it is perhaps the strongest biblical category for understanding the person of Jesus.[3] But even as this revelation is unfolding to his followers, the tension is mounting with those who were still in love with the building and its status and forms—swelling to an unavoidable confrontation.

Confrontation

Jesus is from the beginning closely associated with the Jerusalem temple. He is presented there at forty days old and encounters Simeon and Anna. He is sitting in the temple among the scribes and the teachers at age twelve, reasoning with them. He is attending the temple feasts, teaching in the temple courts, paying the temple tax. He is always acknowl-

---

[3] N. T. Wright, "Jesus' Self-Understanding," originally published in *The Incarnation*, ed. S. T. Davis, D. Kendall, G. O'Collins (Oxford: Oxford University Press, 2002), 56.

edging that it is his Father's house. And yet from early in his ministry he is quick to clarify that the temple is his stage and that he is its superseder—its superior fulfillment. Jesus declared that he was greater than the temple, that he would rebuild in three days the temple they tore down (John explains that he referred to his body), that there would not be one stone of the building left upon another. He claimed preeminence, and he showed it: he now receives the praise and worship; he now gives the law on his own authority; he now grants forgiveness.

With every incident and encounter, the mystified thrill of the people increases, and so does the infuriation of the leadership. The tension builds to a crescendo as Jesus rides into Jerusalem on Palm Sunday. The establishment cringes as the crowds hail Jesus as the great deliverer. What does Jesus do, in this his most public moment? He attacks the temple:

> And Jesus entered the temple and drove out all who sold and bought in the temple, and he overturned the tables of the money-changers and the seats of those who sold pigeons. He said to them, "It is written, 'My house shall be called a house of prayer,' but you make it a den of robbers." And the blind and the lame came to him in the temple, and he healed them. But when the chief priests and the scribes saw the wonderful things that he did, and the children crying out in the temple, "Hosanna to the Son of David!" they were indignant. (Matt. 21:12–15)

Jesus has come to his rightful home, and it has been stolen. So he rushes in forcefully to cleanse his own house. The incarnate temple is enacting the coming judgment on the architectural temple because wickedness has found a prosperous home there. Extortion abounded. Corruption had turned the temple into a business. Many people could not afford to worship God there. The outer court, the only place for the Gentiles to worship, was overrun. It was a chaotic bazaar. The chief priests were barring people from God instead of bringing people to God.

So replay the tape in your mind. Jerusalem is filled with five to six times its normal population because of Passover, like a shopping mall on the day after Thanksgiving. And Jesus comes running into this crowd and begins turning over tables, knocking over benches, pulling the supports out from under booths, opening cages. Money is flying, people are scrambling, animals are squawking. And he is confronting: What have you done with my house? It is filled with greed instead of salvation. My house is supposed to be a haven of prayer and worship for all people, and you are criminally blocking the way! My house, my temple, is a den of robbers! He comes *in* and does not purge Jerusalem from Gentile defilement. He purges the court of the Gentiles from Jewish defilement. He is not attacking their enemies. He's attacking the Jews' greatest point of confidence.

Yet he hasn't come in to judge. He has come in to save. But he must deal with the fraud and the falseness to clear the way for the temple to serve its purpose, which is ultimately to point to Jesus, who says, "Come to me!"

As he stands in the midst of the wreckage, his flashing eyes suddenly soften with tender compassion, because here come the blind and the lame, groping and hobbling their way into the temple to be near him. Jewish authorities barred the disabled from the temple. They were forbidden from entering and offering their sacrifices there. Yet now here they come, limping toward him, and not even bringing a sacrifice. They don't have to. He is the sacrifice. They come with only their need, and he accepts them.

And then there are the children. These nonentities in Jewish society are running loose among the learned elite. And they are the only ones who actually get it—praising Jesus right in his temple. When the chief priests and the scribes saw "the wonderful things that he did," they were "indignant," filled with hatred, murderous hatred (Matt. 21:15). The confrontation is at a fatal impasse, and it breaks his heart. "O Jerusalem, Jerusalem. . . . How often would I have gathered your children together as a hen gathers her brood under her wings, and you would not! See, your house is left to you desolate" (Matt. 23:37–38). What can he do with a people who will come to the temple but will not come to the outstretched arms of God? It is a fatal impasse, and yet Jesus does not run from it. He comes *in* to it, moving from confrontation to culmination.

Culmination

Jesus was not taken to the cross. Jesus went to the cross. His life was not stolen from him. He laid down his life. The glory of the God who was willing to ordain and institute atonement became the glory of the God who will provide atonement. The glory of the God who *is* the atonement. John Stott says that we should never ever wonder why forgiveness is so difficult but rather how is it possible![4] God does not forgive sin. I hope you know that. He can't. He forgives sinners. But sin has to be paid for. Who knew that *this* is what our sin costs? Jesus knew.

---

[4]John Stott, *The Cross of Christ* (Downers Grove, IL: InterVarsity, 1986), 88.

He *knew* it, even as he echoed Solomon's prayer and said, "Father, forgive them." And he knew, because he himself was the answer to that prayer, that the Father would turn away from the next prayer in abandonment, which was required for that forgiveness. The unthinkable extravagance of Jesus the temple! The unimaginable cost to the heart of the Father! *This* is the temple dedication. It is his dedication, not ours.

Glory and forgiveness can be combined only because here they are exchanged. The essence of sin is that I put myself in the place of God, so God put his Son in the place of me. Even as I have taken glory that is not mine, he has taken sin that is not his. Because we have put ourselves where only God deserves to be, he has put himself where only we deserve to be. How *in* is he? He left his rightful throne to take my rightful cross. His is the abandonment, and ours is the embrace. His is the price, and ours is the wealth. "Where is God?" He is on that cross. And, oh, the tear-down! Curtain temple torn from top to bottom.

In this culmination there is full cancellation. Engagement is over at the moment of marriage. Pregnancy is over at the moment of birth. And the temple building is over at the moment he says, "It is finished." There's no more point to it. He is the Word. He is the fulfillment of every jot and tittle of the law. He is the priest. He is the sacrifice. He is the mercy seat. He is the glory. He is the temple. No more building. Atonement and mediation complete. The apostle John speaks of the crucifixion as the glorification of God—the radiance of I'm *in*. This was the glory that was veiled on the cross but exploded into open display in the resurrection. Our temple lives in flesh eternal—flesh that is more permanent than stones, flesh that is more permanent than gold. His is all the glory to have. His is all the forgiveness to give. What do we bring to it? Nothing. Absolutely nothing. It is all from him. It is all completed in him. And it is all for us.

But then he *leaves*. He takes off visibly on a cloud. Yet he has already promised that this ascension is not a disappearance. It is only a departure. It will not mean his absence; it will mean his heightened presence. Again he is making promises over his shoulder—not lesser promises, but bigger promises. Why? Because beyond the Best there is a Better. That's exactly what he says in John 16:7: It is actually better for you that I go away, because then I will *really* come *in*.

Yet their eyes float up, watching him go, and they think, "Come back! Come back!" Not, "Come in!" But his promise is, "I'm *in*." No longer the inhabitant God in a building. No longer only the incarnate God in a body. Now the indwelling God in *our* bodies.

3) THE INDWELLING GOD *IN* OUR BODIES

> When the day of Pentecost arrived, they were all together in one place. And suddenly there came from heaven a sound like a mighty rushing wind, and it filled the entire house where they were sitting. And divided tongues as of fire appeared to them and rested on each one of them. And they were all filled with the Holy Spirit. (Acts 2:1–4)

To the gathering of bewildered believers in that upper room on the day of Pentecost, God came visibly, just like he had in the past, to his former dwelling places. This time he did not come by one big shining cloud appearing to his gathered people but by little glory flames on each of his gathered people. This meant what it has always meant—I'm *in*. In to live and in to stay. The passage doesn't say the room was filled with him. It says *they* were filled with him. What did that make them? What does that make us? It makes us temples of the living God. Jesus had said it, as he told them he was going away: "I will not leave you as orphans; I will come to you." Speaking also of his Father, Jesus said: "We will come to him and make our home with him." Jesus also promised "the Helper, the Holy Spirit, whom the Father will send in my name" (John 14:18, 23, 26). This is not lesser. This is *bigger*. The coming of the Holy Spirit did for this group what nothing had done so far—not three years of Jesus's private teaching, not his miracles, not performing miracles themselves, not witnessing Lazarus raised, not watching Jesus's crucifixion, not even being with the risen Christ. It is *this* day that transforms them.

This is true for us as well. It's not his influence or inspiration or instruction but his indwelling that changes us. We get to say, "Come in!" And he *really* does! "Where is God?" He is in *me*, in a unique, like-nowhere-else, personal way. In to live and in to stay. This is the strangest temple combination of all. More than gold and blood. More even than fully God and fully man. He *in* me and you, and we in him. If you clasp your hands together, is your right hand in your left hand, or your left hand in your right? They are too joined to tell. That's a picture of our union with Christ, and that is the reason the Bible's language flip-flops all the time. We in him. He in us. The presence of his Spirit is so fully his presence that the indwelling of Christ is spoken of as the indwelling of the Spirit, and the indwelling of the Spirit is spoken of as the indwelling of Christ—not because they are compounded or confused but because of their dynamic equivalence. Christ is *in* through his Spirit. The temple is not a nice picture or analogy of what we are. It *is* who we are in union with him.

Facets of Our Templeness

What are the facets of our templeness? Just refer back to the facets of the temple. First, glory. Now, the light of the knowledge of the glory of God shines in *our hearts* in the face of Christ (2 Cor. 4:6). Next, the Word. As before, the glory comes with the Word, which is now given to us as the directions of his love rather than as the life-and-death demands of the law. It is no longer written on tablets of stone, but on our hearts by the Spirit who, we are promised, will teach and remind us of all these things as he guides us into all truth. Third, we are now the site of forgiveness, fully and finally accomplished as our atonement lives in us, through a substitutionary exchange so complete that we have become the righteousness of God. Further, though there is no more blood required in this temple, there are still sacrifices—us, living sacrifices presented as our spiritual act of worship. And the temple is still the place of prayer. We no longer need a building; we have full access to the Father through the indwelling Spirit who translates our prayers, interprets our groaning, and groans for us when we cannot pray anymore.

Finally (a topic for a whole other chapter), the temple is still the place for the congregation or the assembly. The temple is fully who we are as persons, but each of us is not all the temple is. I am defined as the temple. The temple is not defined as me—"I will be your God and you will be my person." That is not the covenant. God promises, "I will be your God, and you will be my *people*." As Ephesians 2 explains, this requires *all* the people—the fullness of all God's people in all places. But it also requires *each* of the people. There are individual aspects of my templeness and yours that the whole needs. Look at the facets of our templeness—the New Testament declarations of who we are. But what about the demands? Those come with the repeated piggy-back language of "fullness."

Fullness of Our Templeness

You know the repeated indicative/imperative language of fullness: you *are* filled with the Spirit—therefore *be* filled with the Spirit. Now, let's get theologically deep for just a moment. What does "filled" mean? My four-year-old can tell you. It means there "ain't no room" for anything else. No more room in our hearts. No more room in our bodies. No more room in our minds. No more room except for God and the me that he is creating. I no longer live; Christ lives in me. We love to camp out on the wonderful truth that we have the fullness of him. But we need to move the campsite to the truth that he is therefore to have the fullness of us. Please hear me. We are never working *for* our templeness. We are never working *toward* our templeness. We can't. In order that we be temples, he has to come in and fill us. But he has! And we must therefore work *from* our templeness. We must reason from it. We must wrestle from it. This is what Paul is constantly doing. Note the order of what he says in 2 Corinthians 6. We *are* the temple of the living God—therefore let us cleanse ourselves, body and spirit, to bring holiness to completion (vv. 16–17).

Paul would never sing:

Oh be careful little eyes what you see.
Oh be careful little ears what you hear.
For the Father up above is looking down in love.
So be careful little feet where you go.

Nice thoughts. Sweet tune. Terribly inadequate theology. So keep the tune. But change the content, and sing with Paul:

Oh be careful, beloved one, to keep your clothes on,
With any but the one who is your spouse.
For you're the very temple of the living God, and *how*
Could you sexually sin with Christ living in your body?

I know that could be a little awkward in preschool Sunday school. But it is the only reality that will transform us. It is not just a Father up above looking down in love. It is the Father and Son living in us by the Spirit. We've got to reason and wrestle from the full implications of his fullness.

Does my watching a particular movie or laughing at a certain YouTube video correspond to my templeness? Does my drinking so much or eating so little square with my templeness? Are my workplace manner and practices directed by my templeness? Does my jealousy and resentment of another demonstrate my templeness? Is my spending so much money, so much time, so much energy, so much conversation, and so much thought on the way that I look determined by my templeness? Can social superiority, racial superiority, or spiritual superiority coexist with my templeness? Does our very living deny our templeness?

We're warned about it in Titus 1:16: "They profess to know

God, but they deny him by their works." How *in* is he? He is so in that the God who came with eyes and ears and hands and feet is to fill our seeing and our hearing and our doing and our spending and our going and our thinking. There is no place for the attitude that what I do with my money and my body and my work and my relationships is up to me as long as my heart is fully committed to Jesus. *None* of it is up to me, because He fills *all* of it. The Spirit is *in* me to tell me who Christ is but also to tell me who I really am, and to provide everything for me in Christ actually to become that person. And we can be confident about the fullness of our templeness because of the force of our templeness.

Force of Our Templeness

Look again at *who* is in us: "You . . . are not in the flesh; you are in the Spirit. . . . If the Spirit of him who raised Jesus from the dead dwells in you, he who raised Christ Jesus from the dead will also give life to your mortal bodies through his Spirit who dwells in you" (Rom. 8:9, 11). How powerful is the force of his presence? Who raised Jesus from the dead? He who is at work in us. He is the guarantee of our own physical resurrection. Have you ever seen a body in a coffin? He is going to bring *that* body back to life. So reason from the greater to the lesser: if he can overcome my death, don't I know that he can overcome my habits? My temptations? My fears? My flesh?

Yes, there is Spirit-flesh warfare, but he is greater, and he *will* progressively win. Not only will we see more and more of his glory but also, from his *in*-ness, *we* are being transformed from one degree of glory to another. We have moved in the history of redemption from the glory that is shown to the glory that is *shared*. We are, as Scripture says, "filled with all the fullness of God" (Eph. 3:19).

As we rejoice in the certainty of our templeness, and as we work from the confidence of our templeness, we know that even this templeness is not permanent. Our "Come in!" is not the final word. His indwelling is not our final state. Even this is a preparation. There is still a leaning and a longing because beyond the Best there is a Better. He is still *really* coming. The inhabitant God in a building, the incarnate God in a body, the indwelling God in our bodies will come as the inviting God.

4) THE INVITING GOD

His word to us is the final word. It is that which we live to hear. What is it? What will he say to us? "Come *in*!" The Lord of glory does not wait for us. He doesn't beckon us. He doesn't send for us. He *comes* for us. I AM comes for us. I'm *in* comes for us with outstretched arms and says, *"You're in!"* His work will be so complete in us that we are complete, glorified. No more veils. No more clouds. No more dim vision. *No more temple.* We will see him as he is. We will be like him. We will be eternally with him, living with him, on his throne and in his lap.

My grandparents loved their new pastor and his family. He had been serving the church in the small Mississippi town for only a couple of years when his wife was diagnosed with a brain tumor that quickly took her from him and their four young children. During her illness, when she was already very frail, she walked through the town square into the floral shop owned by church members. They felt awkward as she entered, because they were working on big, beautiful sprays of flowers for a funeral that afternoon. They looked at her with pained smiles as she greeted them very brightly. She walked right over to the counter, looked through the cards, picked one, and put her arm around her friend as she said, "This is the card I want on all my funeral flowers." It read, "Welcome to your new home."

Jesus says, I am coming again, for one reason: that where I am you may be also—forever *in* with him who is our eternal home.

REFLECTION AND DISCUSSION QUESTIONS

1) God shows himself to his people—spectacularly!—in 1 Kings 8. Sum up what the people see and what God is showing about himself.

2) How does what we learn of God in 1 Kings 8 both build on and add to the revelation we saw in Exodus 19?

3) Solomon speaks many wise words in 1 Kings 8. List some of the key truths about God that he acknowledges in his words to Israel and to the Lord.

4) Paige Brown took us on a quick "aerial study" of the Bible's temple theme. In a few sentences, sum up that trip and its climactic destination in the New Testament.

5) How do you respond to this temple scene and this temple theme? If *this is your God*, what difference might that make to you today or tomorrow, both in your communion with God and in your interaction with others?

3

In the Throne Room

THE GOD OF HOLINESS AND HOPE

Isaiah 6

JOHN PIPER

On June 1, 1973, Chuck Colson, special counsel to President Nixon, heard the gospel from Tom Phillips, while Watergate exploded in the press. That night, as Colson describes it, "I cried out to God and found myself drawn irresistibly into his waiting arms. That was the night I gave my life to Jesus Christ and began the greatest adventure of my life."[1] Several years later the former White House hatchet man repented of a woefully inadequate view of God. He was in a very dry season. A friend suggested to Colson that he watch a videocassette lecture series by R. C. Sproul on the holiness of God. Here's what Colson writes in his book *Loving God*:

---

[1] Charles Colson, *Loving God* (Grand Rapids, MI: Zondervan, 1996), 247.

By the end of the sixth lecture I was on my knees, deep in prayer, in awe of God's absolute holiness. It was a life-changing experience as I gained a completely new understanding of the holy God I believe in and worship.[2]

The same things happened to Job: He was blameless and upright, one who feared God and turned away from evil (Job 1:1). What more did he need? But after great suffering, and great wrestlings with God, the Lord appeared to him:

> Will you even put me in the wrong?
>   Will you condemn me that you may be in the right?
> Have you an arm like God,
>   and can you thunder with a voice like his?
> Adorn yourself with majesty and dignity;
>   clothe yourself with glory and splendor.
> Pour out the overflowings of your anger,
>   and look on everyone who is proud and abase him.
> Look on everyone who is proud and bring him low
>   and tread down the wicked where they stand.
>   (40:8–12)

In the end Job, like Colson, came to a "completely new understanding of the holy God." He said:

> Therefore I have uttered what I did not understand,
>   things too wonderful for me, which I did not
>   know. . . .
> I had heard of you by the hearing of the ear,
>   but now my eye sees you;
> therefore I despise myself
>   and repent in dust and ashes. (42:3–6)

---

[2] Ibid., 15.

And it happened to Isaiah. After God appeared to him (Isa. 6:1–4), he said:

> Woe is me! For I am lost; for I am a man of unclean lips, and I dwell in the midst of a people of unclean lips; for my eyes have seen the King, the LORD of hosts! (v. 5)

This has happened to many of us. It happened to me between my twenty-second and twenty-fifth year—a new understanding of the holy God, a taste for the majesty of God. May the Lord do it for you from Isaiah 6. Or if you already have this taste, may the Lord satisfy your soul with this vision more deeply than ever before.

Isaiah invites us to share his vision of God:

> In the year that King Uzziah died I saw the Lord sitting upon a throne, high and lifted up; and the train of his robe filled the temple. Above him stood the seraphim. Each had six wings: with two he covered his face, and with two he covered his feet, and with two he flew. And one called to another and said:
>
> > "Holy, holy, holy is the LORD of hosts;
> > the whole earth is full of his glory!"
>
> And the foundations of the thresholds shook at the voice of him who called, and the house was filled with smoke. (6:1–4)

I see at least seven glimpses of God in these four verses.

GLIMPSE 1: GOD IS ALIVE

First, God is *alive*. "In the year that King Uzziah died . . ." Uzziah is dead, but God lives on. "From everlasting to everlasting you are God" (Ps. 90:2). God was the living God when this universe came into existence. He was the living God when Socrates drank his poison. He was the living God when William Bradford governed Plymouth Colony. He was the living God in 1966 when Thomas Altizer proclaimed him dead and *Time* magazine put it on the front cover. And he will be the living God ten trillion ages from now when all the puny potshots against his reality will have sunk into oblivion like BBs at the bottom of the Pacific Ocean.

"In the year that King Uzziah died I saw the Lord." There is not a single head of state in all the world who will be there in fifty years. The turnover in world leadership is 100 percent, but there is no turnover in the Trinity. He never had a beginning and therefore depends on nothing for his existence. He always has been and always will be alive.

GLIMPSE 2: GOD IS AUTHORITATIVE

Second, God is *authoritative*. "I saw the Lord sitting upon a *throne*." No vision of heaven has ever caught a glimpse of God plowing a field or cutting his grass or shining shoes or filling out reports or loading a truck. Heaven is not coming apart at the seams by inattention. God is never at wits' end with his heavenly realm. He sits. And he sits on a *throne*. All is at peace, and he has control.

The throne is his right to rule the world. We do not give God authority over our lives. He has it, whether we like it or not. What utter folly to act as though we had any rights to call God into question! Few things are more humbling, few things give us that sense of raw majesty, as does the truth that God is utterly *authoritative*. He is the Supreme Court, the

Legislature, and the Chief Executive. After him, there is no appeal.

GLIMPSE 3: GOD IS OMNIPOTENT

Third, God is *omnipotent*. The throne of his authority is not one among many. It is high and lifted up. "I saw the Lord sitting upon a throne, high and lifted up." That God's throne is higher than every other throne signifies God's superior power to exercise his authority. No opposing authority can nullify the decrees of God. What he purposes, he accomplishes. "My counsel shall stand, and I will accomplish all my purpose" (Isa. 46:10). "He does according to his will among the host of heaven and among the inhabitants of the earth; and none can stay his hand" (Dan. 4:35). And this omnipotent authority of the living God is a refuge full of joy and power for those who keep his covenant.

GLIMPSE 4: GOD IS RESPLENDENT

Fourth, God is *resplendent*. "I saw the Lord sitting upon a throne, high and lifted up; *and the train of his robe filled the temple.*" You have seen pictures of brides whose dresses are gathered around them covering the steps and the platform. What would the meaning be if the train filled the aisles and covered the seats and the choir loft, woven all of one piece? That God's robe fills the entire heavenly temple means that he is a God of incomparable splendor. The fullness of God's splendor shows itself in a thousand ways.

I used to read *Ranger Rick* magazine. I recall an article on species of fish who live deep in the dark sea and have their own built-in lights. Some have lamps hanging from their chins, some have luminescent noses, and some have beacons under their eyes. There are a thousand kinds of self-lighted fish that live deep in the ocean where none of us can see and marvel. They are spectacularly weird and beautiful. Why are they there? Why not just a dozen or so efficient, streamlined models? Because God is lavish in splendor. His creative fullness spills over in excessive beauty. And if that's the way the world is, how much more resplendent must be the Lord who thought it up and made it?

GLIMPSE 5: GOD IS REVERED

Fifth, God is *revered*. "Above him stood the seraphim. Each had six wings: with two he covered his face, and with two he covered his feet, and with two he flew" (v. 2). No one knows what these strange six-winged creatures with feet and eyes and intelligence are. They never appear again in the Bible—at least not under the name "seraphim." Given the grandeur of the scene and the power of the angelic hosts, we had best not picture chubby, winged babies fluttering about the Lord's ears. According to Isaiah 6:4, when one of them speaks, the foundations of the temple shake. We would do better to think of the Blue Angels—those four jets that fly in formation—*diving* in formation before the presidential entourage and cracking the sound barrier just before his face. There are no puny or silly creatures in heaven. Only magnificent ones.

And the point is: not even they can look upon the Lord, nor do they feel worthy even to leave their feet exposed in his presence. Great and good as they are, untainted by human sin, they revere their Maker in great humility. An angel terrifies a man with his brilliance and power. But angels themselves hide in holy fear and reverence from the splendor of God. He is continually revered.

GLIMPSE 6: GOD IS HOLY

Sixth, God is *holy*. "And one called to another and said: 'Holy, holy, holy is the LORD of hosts'" (v. 3). Language is pushing its limits of usefulness here. The effort to define the holiness of God ultimately winds up saying: God is *holy* means God is *God*.

Let me illustrate. The root meaning of *holy* is probably "to cut or separate." A *holy thing* is cut off from and separated from common (we would say "secular") use. Earthly things and persons are holy as they are distinct from the world and devoted to God. So the Bible speaks of holy ground (Ex. 3:5), holy assemblies (Ex. 12:16), holy sabbaths (Ex. 16:23), a holy nation (Ex. 19:6), holy garments (Ex. 28:2), a holy city (Neh. 11:1), holy promises (Ps. 105:42), holy men (2 Pet. 1:21) and women (1 Pet. 3:5), holy Scriptures (2 Tim. 3:15), holy hands (1 Tim. 2:8), a holy kiss (Rom. 16:16), and a holy faith (Jude 20). Almost anything can become holy if it is separated from the common and devoted to God.

But notice what happens when this definition is applied to God himself. From what can you separate God to make him holy? The very god-ness of God means that he is separate from all that is not God. There is an infinite, qualitative difference between Creator and creature. God is one of a kind. Sui generis—in a class by himself. In that sense he is utterly holy. But then you have said no more than that he is God.

Or, if the holiness of a man derives from being separated

from the world and devoted to God, to whom is God devoted so as to derive his holiness? To no one but himself. It is blasphemy to say that there is a higher reality than God to which he must conform in order to be holy. God is the absolute reality beyond which is only more of God. When asked for his name in Exodus 3:14, he said, "I AM WHO I AM." His being and his character are utterly undetermined by anything outside himself. He is not holy because he keeps the rules. He wrote the rules! God is not holy because he keeps the law. The law is holy because it reveals God. God is absolute. Everything else is derivative.

What then is his holiness? His holiness is his utterly unique divine, transcendent, pure essence, which in his uniqueness has infinite value. It determines all that he is and does and is determined by no one. His holiness is what he is as God, which no one else is or ever will be. Call it his majesty, his divinity, his supreme greatness, his value as the pearl of great price.

In the end, language runs out. In the word *holy* we have sailed to the world's end in the utter silence of reverence and wonder and awe. "The LORD is in his *holy* temple; let all the earth keep silence before him" (Hab. 2:20).

GLIMPSE 7: GOD IS GLORIOUS

But before the silence and the shaking of the foundations and the all-concealing smoke, we learn a seventh final thing about God: God is glorious. "Holy, holy, holy is the LORD of hosts; the whole earth is full of his glory!"

The glory of God is the manifestation of his holiness. God's holiness is the incomparable perfection of his divine nature;

his glory is the display of that holiness. "God is glorious" means: God's holiness has gone public. His glory is the open revelation of the secret of his holiness. In Leviticus 10:3 God says, "I will show myself *holy* among those who are near me, and before all the people I will be *glorified*" (RSV). When God shows himself to be holy, what we see is glory. The holiness of God is his concealed glory. The glory of God is his revealed holiness.

THE GLIMPSES POINT AHEAD

Now, what does this have to do with Jesus Christ incarnate as the God-man crucified and risen from the dead at the center of history?

The Gospel of John makes the connections for us more clearly than anyone, in John 12. I will put it in a very brief statement. In Isaiah 6, Isaiah presents God as high and holy and majestic and authoritative and sovereign and resplendent, and God says in verse 10 that this message will harden the people. They do not want such a God. But the chapter ends with a reference to a stump of faithfulness that remains, and Isaiah speaks of a "holy seed" (v. 13).

In Isaiah 53 that seed is described as the suffering servant who had "no form or majesty that we should look at him, and no beauty that we should desire him. He was despised and rejected by men" (vv. 2–3). This is just the opposite of the picture of God in Isaiah 6.

But Isaiah 53:1 says they rejected that message as well: "Who has believed what he has heard from us?"

These are the very two texts that John quotes in reference to the rejection of Jesus in John 12:38 and 12:40. Why? John tells us in John 12:41: "Isaiah said these things because he saw his glory and spoke of him." Isaiah saw the glory of Christ.

In other words, Jesus was the fulfillment of both the majesty of Isaiah 6 and the misery of Isaiah 53. And that, John says, is why Jesus was rejected. He came to his own, and his own did not receive him. Why? Because Jesus was the glory of Isaiah 6 and the suffering servant of Isaiah 53. John says so in John 12:41: "Isaiah said these things because he saw his glory and spoke of him."

We beheld his glory, glory of the only Son from the Father full of grace and truth, and that glory was the unprecedented mingling of the majesty of Isaiah 6 and the misery of Isaiah 53. And why was this incomparable Christ rejected? John gives the answer in John 12:43: The people "loved the glory that comes from man more than the glory that comes from God."

And because they loved human glory more than divine glory they rejected Jesus—the embodiment of the glory of God, both in his greatness as God and his lowliness as the suffering servant.

But all this was part of God's design. "The Son of Man came not to be served but to serve, and to give his life as a ransom for many" (Mark 10:45). His rejection was the plan because his death for sinners was the plan.

Does he then abandon his people Israel because they rejected him? No. That too is part of the plan. "A partial hardening has come upon Israel, until the fullness of the Gentiles has come in. And in this way all Israel will be saved" (Rom. 11:25–26).

Or as Romans 11:31 says concerning Israel: "They too have

now been disobedient in order that by the mercy shown to you [Gentiles] they also may now receive mercy." Nothing has been wasted. There were no detours on the way to this great salvation of all God's elect.

When Paul stands back and looks at the whole plan, he worships:

Oh, the depth of the riches and wisdom and knowledge of God! How unsearchable are his judgments and how inscrutable his ways!

"For who has known the mind of the Lord,
or who has been his counselor?"
"Or who has given a gift to him
that he might be repaid?"

For from him and through him and to him are all things. To him be glory forever. Amen. (Rom. 11:33–36)

Here is our God.

REFLECTION AND DISCUSSION QUESTIONS

1) "I saw the Lord," says the prophet Isaiah. How is this appearance of God similar to and yet different from the previous appearances we have seen (Exodus 19 and 1 Kings 8)?

2) How does Isaiah 6:1–4 provide the foundation and explanation for each subsequent part of Isaiah 6?

3) To show the relation of Isaiah 6 to Jesus Christ, John Piper leads us first to Isaiah 53 and then to John 12. How beautiful is the whole of God's Word! Summarize the way these passages together reveal Christ to us.

4) Isaiah 6 shows not just God's revelation but also Isaiah's responses—and God's responses to Isaiah's responses! What further truths about God are revealed as he deals with Isaiah throughout this scene?

5) Review John Piper's seven glimpses of God from Isaiah 6 and review the details in the biblical text. Why do God's people need to carry these glimpses with us into our prayers, our worship, and our everyday lives? What difference will these glimpses make?

4

From a Miry Swamp

THE GOD WHO COMES AND DELIVERS

Psalm 40

CARRIE SANDOM

Emily had never meant to have an affair but when the opportunity presented itself, she fell headlong into an adulterous
relationship. She had been a Christian for many years, but
despite a couple of long-term relationships with men, she
had never married. She found that the struggle with singleness was very acute at times, especially as most of her friends
were now settling down and starting to have children. She
pretended she was fine about it and buried herself in her ca-
reer, finding a certain degree of satisfaction from the financial
freedom it gave her.

Jack was one of the junior partners in her law firm. He
was fun and good-looking, but he was not a Christian. He
was married, but his wife of seven years was apparently very

preoccupied with their two young children and no longer gave him any attention. At least, that's what Jack said. What Emily thought was a bit of harmless flirting in the office had become an occasional drink after work and then a regular heart-to-heart over dinner. Looking back, Emily realized that these illicit encounters with him had been a rather childish attempt to prove to herself that marriage was awful and she was better off on her own. But then she began to reason with herself that spending time with him was not a bad thing to do. His wife clearly wasn't interested in him anymore, and he was always so charming, so attentive, so understanding, so tender. And so, somehow, she had ended up sleeping with him, not just once, but several times. At first the guilt had almost completely overwhelmed her, but after a while it wasn't as difficult to live with as it had been—and that's what really scares her now. She is ensnared, and she knows it.

Joan had made a commitment to the Lord seventy years ago and had served in the children's Sunday school for over forty years. She had lost count of the number of children she had taught during that time, but they had all loved her, affectionately calling her "Miss Joan." But that was a long time ago. In recent years Joan's health has started to deteriorate. First it was her eyes, then it was her back, then it was her knees, and now it is her heart. She has been seeing four different hospital consultants and has lost track of the number of appointments she has been to. Her health has become so all-consuming that it is all she ever talks about. Friends of hers from church used to visit her, but they have found it increasingly hard to engage with her because every conversation comes back to the issue of her health and the list of her ailments. She has exhausted them so much that, one by one, they have stopped coming. This has disgruntled Joan enormously, and she has begun to feel very resentful. After all she has done for the church over the years, it seems nobody really cares about her. She dwells on this thought and turns it over and over in her mind. Joan is a bitter old woman who has become consumed by an unhealthy self-absorption.

Kate loves her husband and her children, but she knows that her faith in Christ isn't growing anymore. Everything she does seems to revolve around the children—getting them to school in the morning, then collecting them in the afternoon and taking them to ballet classes, trumpet lessons, and football practice. She stopped reading her Bible some months ago and, although she still prays every day (usually a quick arrow prayer on her way to something else), she knows she isn't pressing on in her faith as she once was.

It was during her college days that her faith in the Lord had grown the most. Talking about Jesus to her friends seemed very easy back then. Her enthusiasm to serve the Lord had taken her on two short-term mission trips to South America, and she had loved getting to know the other members of the team and the missionaries who hosted them. The prayer and praise meetings had lasted for several hours, but nobody had really noticed the time. The fellowship she had enjoyed had been so warm, so encouraging, and so inspiring—but that was a long time ago, and Kate's heart has grown cold.

What these three women have in common is that they are all stuck in a miry swamp, a deep pit of despair, and they are rapidly sinking into the sludge at the bottom of it. For sure, they are there for very different reasons: one is compromised, one is consumed, and the other is coldhearted. But they are in a deep pit all the same, and their situations seem utterly hopeless. But, of course, they aren't the only ones. Many of us have been in miry swamps like these—and maybe some of us are still there. Whether it's because of the relentless expectations of our boss or the long-term illness of a loved one; whether we're being consumed and overtaken by money, or power, or exercise, or our body shape; whether we're wrestling with pride or gossip or acquisitiveness—we all know what it's like to be stuck in a miry swamp. It seems the more we try to get ourselves out, the more ensnared we become.

But the Lord does not want us to wallow in a pit of disobedience, gloom, or despondency. Various Scriptures testify to that fact. For example, in the Psalms he has given us a wide range of human predicaments and how to respond to them, and being in a pit of despair (or a miry bog, as it is sometimes described) is just one of them. Of course, the Psalms themselves are a collection of songs and hymns that the nation of Israel sang as they gathered in their family groups to listen to the Word of God and celebrate various festivals together. They were written primarily to teach them about God: his character and his purposes in the world, who he is, what he does, and how he relates to his people. But the psalms also showed them how they were to respond to him in all the different situations of life.

Psalm 40 is one of the many psalms written by David, Israel's greatest king. Perhaps surprisingly, in this psalm we find him in a deep pit of gloom and despair. Verse 12 explains why David is feeling so low:

For evils have encompassed me
    beyond number;
my iniquities have overtaken me,
    and I cannot see;
they are more than the hairs of my head;
    my heart fails me.

David is aware of his many sins, sins that have ensnared and overwhelmed him. We are not told in detail what these sins are, but David knows they are numerous. What's more, they have overwhelmed him so that he cannot see straight, and his heart has grown faint. But his many sins are not the only thing troubling him. He also has external pressures from his enemies, who are seeking his downfall. We see this in verse 14:

Let those be put to shame and disappointed altogether
    who seek to snatch away my life;
let those be turned back and brought to dishonor
    who delight in my hurt!

Whichever way you look at it, David's situation is pretty desperate and he can see no way out of it. So what does he do? What does he remember about God? What does he pray for? And how does this help us today? The psalm falls neatly into two sections.

1) DAVID REMEMBERS GOD'S DELIVERANCE IN THE PAST (PS. 40:1–10)

David calls to mind another time when he was in a miry bog of despair. The circumstances that led to this are not spelled out, perhaps for good reason, as we might get distracted by them. David remembers the desperation he felt, the cries he uttered, and the long wait he endured, but he doesn't dwell on any of these. Instead his focus is on the Lord, who delivered him:

> I waited patiently for the LORD;
>   he inclined to me and heard my cry.
> He drew me up from the pit of destruction,
>   out of the miry bog,
> and set my feet upon a rock,
>   making my steps secure.
> He put a new song in my mouth,
>   a song of praise to our God.
> Many will see and fear,
>   and put their trust in the LORD. (vv. 1–3)

The word "LORD" appears in capital letters, as it does in many passages throughout the Old Testament. This is the covenant name for God—Yahweh—a name first revealed to Moses at the burning bush, when God promised to deliver his people from Egypt (Exodus 3). Some three hundred years later, David speaks to "the LORD" from within the context of his own covenant relationship and recalls how he too was once delivered by this same "LORD." It's as though David preaches to himself about what God has done for him in the past. He remembers how Yahweh's deliverance came in stages:

> Verse 1: "He *inclined to me* [literally he stooped down to listen to me] and heard my cry." Like that of a parent reaching out to console his distraught child, the Lord's gracious intervention stands out to David.

> Verse 2: "He *drew me up* from the pit of destruction, out of the miry bog." There was no way David could get himself

out of such a hole. It was the Lord's initiative, and his alone. Only the Lord could deliver him.

Verse 2: He "*set my feet* upon a rock, making my steps secure." The Lord pulled him out of the miry swamp, where he was sinking fast, and put his feet on solid ground, where he could stand firm.

Verse 3: "He *put a new song* in my mouth, a song of praise to our God." The Lord's rescue lifted David's whole being— his body, mind, and spirit—and put a new song of praise in his heart.

Notice, too, that it is a song of praise to "our" God, not just to "my" God. David knows that this is what Yahweh has promised to do for all his people. In Moses's generation, the whole covenant community experienced the wonder of the Lord's deliverance from Egypt. It is part of God's nature to deliver those who call on his name and put their trust in him. This is David's God; this is Israel's God. He is the God who delivers. He reveals himself to be a God of mercy who delights in rescuing his people. Note too, at the end of verse 3, how David anticipates that many others will come to know of the Lord's deliverance and put their trust in him. Now, some people may find it hard to identify with what David is saying here, maybe because they have never been in a particularly desperate situation. But those of us who know what it is like to be utterly helpless and then wonderfully rescued will know something of the joy that David felt.

I was four years old when I found myself in an utterly desperate situation, one that even now gives me goose bumps when I think about it. I was learning to swim, and my mother had drummed into me that when I was in the pool, I was never to go out of my depth. I was old enough to understand that if I went beyond my depth and got into trouble, then I wouldn't be able to put my feet down on the floor to steady myself—and not being able to stand would lead only to further panic.

Well, you can guess what happened. Whether it was my foolish pride or just a careless mistake, I don't remember. But one afternoon I was swimming in the pool and wandered out of my depth. The wave of terror that came over me was unbelievably powerful as I tried, in vain, to put my feet on the bottom. I began to scream, but that meant I also started to swallow water. The fear of not being able to swim was now overtaken by the fear of not being able to breathe, and I began to thrash about in the water—screaming, spluttering, and gasping for breath.

It felt like an eternity to me, but it can only have been a few moments before my father, who was swimming at the other end of the pool, came over to where I was, pulled me out of the water, and handed me to my mother, who was waiting anxiously by the side of the pool. The relief of being back on firm ground was immediate, and the security of my mother's embrace brought great comfort, but it took a good while for my breathing to return to normal and several years before I would overcome my fear of the water. As for my dad? Well, he teased me for a long time about the bruises I gave him as I thrashed about in the water, but nothing he said could stop me from believing that he was a real hero that afternoon, and no amount of provocation could ever undermine the relief and gratitude I felt for my rescue.

Even if we cannot personally imagine a particularly desperate situation that brought a dramatic rescue, there was one played out in front of millions of people not so long ago. In August 2010, thirty-three miners at the San José copper mine near Copiapó in northern Chile were trapped underground for sixty-nine days. For the first seventeen days of their captivity, nobody knew if they were even alive. The miners themselves, trapped some seven hundred meters (almost one-half mile) below the surface of the mine when the mineshaft collapsed, did not know if anyone would reach them before they suffocated or died from thirst. Their situation was utterly hopeless. But, remarkably, sixty-nine days later, and under the gaze of the watching world, all thirty-three miners were brought back to the surface unharmed. Rescued from the depths of the earth and miraculously reunited with their loved ones, it's no wonder they knelt down and prayed to God—who had saved them against all the odds.

David remembers how the Lord delivered him and put a new song of praise in his mouth. But that's not all we learn here. The wonder of the Lord's deliverance prompted David to respond in three ways. First, as we see in verses 4 and 5, *he affirmed his faith in God*:

> Blessed is the man who makes
>   the LORD his trust,
> who does not turn to the proud,
>   to those who go astray after a lie!
> You have multiplied, O LORD my God,
>   your wondrous deeds and your thoughts toward us;
>   none can compare with you!
> I will proclaim and tell of them,
>   yet they are more than can be told.

David affirmed his belief that God's favor rests on those who put their trust in him, who do not turn to the proud or follow after false gods. Nothing the world offers can compare with the Lord God of Israel, who has done marvelous deeds and revealed his good purposes to his people. No one can number them; no one could ever match them.

David surely has in mind here not just the personal deliverance he received but also the mighty wonders of God throughout Israel's history: when he rescued Noah and his family from the flood (Genesis 6–9); when he delivered his servant Joseph from wrongful imprisonment in Egypt (Genesis 41); and, supremely, when he redeemed his people Israel from slavery (Exodus 12) and brought them safely to the Promised Land (Joshua 3). David affirmed his faith in God. But that's not all.

Second, David *dedicated himself to God's will* (Ps. 40:6–8):

> In sacrifice and offering you have not delighted,
>   but you have given me an open ear.
> Burnt offering and sin offering
>   you have not required.
> Then I said, "Behold, I have come;
>   in the scroll of the book it is written of me:
> I delight to do your will, O my God;
>   your law is within my heart."

The phrase "you have given me an open ear" in verse 6 (or, in some versions, "you have pierced my ears") is more literally translated "you have dug out my ears." David understands that God has opened up the channels so that he can hear him clearly. He realizes that the Lord doesn't delight in formal

ceremonies or external religion. He does not want burnt offerings and sin offerings. What he wants instead is a heart full
of devotion with an inner resolve to be obedient.

So David dedicated himself to serve the Lord in this way.
He said, "Behold, I have come . . . to do your will"—a bold
statement that speaks of his desire to be obedient. He wants
nothing other than God's law to be written on his heart and
longs that his life might be shaped by total submission to God's
will. This desire to be obedient is not uncommon when people
have received God's deliverance. Indeed, some would say the
desire to live an obedient life is a mark of true conversion. The
Puritans certainly thought so, as this prayer from *The Valley of
Vision*, a collection of Puritan prayers and devotions, reveals:

> Thou hast struck a heavy blow at my pride,
> at the false god of self,
> and I lie in pieces before thee.
> But thou hast given me another Master and Lord,
> thy Son, Jesus,
> and now my heart is turned towards holiness,
> my life speeds as an arrow from a bow
> towards complete obedience to thee.[1]

In light of the Lord's deliverance, David affirmed his faith
in God, he dedicated himself to God's will, and, third, he *proclaimed God's Word* (vv. 9–10):

> I have told the glad news of deliverance
>   in the great congregation;
>   behold, I have not restrained my lips,

---

[1] From "Heart Corruptions," in *The Valley of Vision: A Collection of Puritan Prayers and Devotions*, ed. Arthur Bennett (Carlisle, PA: Banner of Truth, 1975), 130–31.

as you know, O LORD.
I have not hidden your deliverance within my heart;
    I have spoken of your faithfulness and your salvation;
I have not concealed your steadfast love and your
      faithfulness
from the great congregation.

David recalls how he proclaimed the Lord's deliverance to all people, and he calls on the Lord himself as a witness. To stress this fact, David uses the negatives to underline the positives: "I *have not* restrained my lips. . . . I *have not* hidden your deliverance within my heart. . . . I *have not* concealed your steadfast love." But "I *have* told the glad news of deliverance. . . . I *have* spoken of your faithfulness and your salvation."

David remembers that God lifted him out of the miry pit and set his feet back on firm ground. And it is *this* deliverance in the past that gives him the ongoing confidence we see in the second half of the psalm.

2) DAVID PRAYS FOR GOD'S DELIVERANCE IN THE PRESENT (PS. 40:11–17)

Verse 11 is the hinge between the two sections of Psalm 40:

As for you, O LORD, you will not restrain
    your mercy from me;
your steadfast love and your faithfulness will
    ever preserve me!

Up until this point David has been remembering God's deliverance in the past and the response he made to that deliverance. But David's situation has changed. He is once again in a miry pit, but remembering God's goodness in the past gives him confidence as he now prays for God's deliverance in the present.

We have seen already how desperate David's situation has become. He's fighting battles on two fronts: inside and out. The internal battle, with his own sin, has become too great. His iniquities have overtaken him, and he has been ensnared (v. 12). His desire to be obedient to God's will was well-meant, but it had been short-lived: his flesh is weak and his heart has failed. But that's not all.

The external battles are raging all around him as well (v. 14). He is surrounded by his enemies, who are seeking his downfall. He was God's anointed king, but throughout his reign he was opposed by many people—both inside and outside of Israel—who sought his ruin and destruction.

David's situation is once again very bleak. He has been humbled by his sin, and he is being pursued by evil men. He acknowledges his utter helplessness and cries out to the Lord. As he does so, he lifts his attention off himself and onto the Lord, focusing on two things in particular—first, the Lord's unchanging character. God's mercy never fails (v. 11):

> As for you, O LORD, you will not restrain
>   your mercy from me;
> your steadfast love and your faithfulness will
>   ever preserve me!

The Lord is always faithful to himself. He is merciful, and his steadfast love will protect and preserve his people. David prays with confidence, knowing that the Lord doesn't change. He showed his mercy to David in the past, and he will be merciful again. David prays with confidence not only because of the Lord's unchanging character but also because of *the Lord's enduring promise*. His deliverance will come (vv. 16–17):

> But may all who seek you
>   rejoice and be glad in you;
> may those who love your salvation
>   say continually, "Great is the LORD!"
> As for me, I am poor and needy,
>   but the Lord takes thought for me.
> You are my help and my deliverer;
>   do not delay, O my God!

David knows from past experience that the Lord listens to the cries of his people. All those who seek him will rejoice and be glad in him because one day his salvation will come! David acknowledges the frailty of his situation once again—he is poor and in need—but he knows the Lord is mindful of his people. His deliverance will come.

The psalm ends in verse 17 with a final declaration of faith and a prayer:

> You are my help and my deliverer;
>   do not delay, O my God!

David cries out to the Lord from the depths. He is ensnared by sin and in fear for his life. Encouraged by the knowledge of God's deliverance in the past, he prays for God's deliverance in the present. And then he waits, confident that the Lord's mercy never fails and his deliverance will one day come.

3) WE FIND GOD'S DELIVERANCE NOW

That is a wonderful passage and would have been a great encouragement to the people of Israel as they sang it at their family gatherings and festivals. But what does this psalm, written over three thousand years ago, have to say to us today? We need to remember that, compared to David, we stand in a very different historical context; but this means that ultimately we have *even more reason* to trust in the Lord and *even more reason* for confidence.

I said at the beginning that the psalms were written to teach us about God and how we should respond to him—and this psalm does both of these things. But after the resurrection Jesus revealed to his disciples that there is *even more treasure* to be found in the psalms, as they point us forward to him.

> Then [Jesus] said to them, "These are my words that I spoke to you while I was still with you, that everything written about me in the Law of Moses and the Prophets and the Psalms must be fulfilled." Then he opened their minds to understand the Scriptures. (Luke 24:44–45)

Jesus revealed that the Old Testament doesn't just teach us about God and how to respond to him, but it actually points forward to all that he will do through his Son. Many of the psalms are then interpreted by the New Testament writers in light of this revelation and used to show how they point forward to the Lord Jesus.

The letter to the Hebrews provides us with numerous examples of this. The Hebrews were a bunch of Christian believers, but they were not in a very good way. Disillusioned by how hard it was to be Christians in an increasingly hostile culture, they were tempted to go back to Judaism. The writer pleads with them not to abandon the Lord Jesus, because he is better than anything Judaism has to offer. He is a better leader than Moses and a better priest than Aaron; he establishes a better covenant based on better promises. But that's not all. The writer reminds them that animal sacrifices could never deal with sin, and therefore something else was needed if their sins were to be atoned for. Here is what he says in Hebrews 10:

> For it is impossible for the blood of bulls and goats to take away sins. Consequently, when Christ came into the world, he said,
>
> "Sacrifices and offerings you have not desired,
>   but a body have you prepared for me;
> in burnt offerings and sin offerings
>   you have taken no pleasure.
> Then I said, 'Behold, I have come to do your will,
>   O God,
>   as it is written of me in the scroll of the book.'"
>   (vv. 4–7)

I wonder if that reminds you of anything? Yes, it's Psalm 40! This is what David had said all those years ago: that he had come to do God's will—but he *couldn't do it!* Sin had too strong a hold on him, and he failed. He couldn't obey God's will for long, any more than you or I can. He needed a Savior, one who could deal with his sin once and for all.

Does that remind you of anyone? Yes, of course—the Lord Jesus. *He* is the one who comes, and *he* is the one who delivers. It was impossible for the blood of bulls and goats to take away sins. The law demanded that they were offered for a time, but they couldn't deal with the real problem—the problem of the human heart. So the Lord God prepared a body for the Lord Jesus. He was the *one true servant*, who always did his Father's will, and *the one true sacrifice*, who dealt with sin forever. Jesus died on the cross and took upon himself the punishment that we deserve. It was a *substitutionary* death: he died in our place. And it was a *sacrificial* death: he died for our sins. He died the death that you and I deserve, and he lived the perfect life that you and I could never live. And by his Spirit, his law is now written on our hearts, enabling us to live a life of obedience. Only Jesus could do this. He is the one David was speaking of in Psalm 40—although he probably didn't know it at the time. Jesus is the one who finally brought the Lord's deliverance. And so we have even more reason to trust in him. His mercy never fails, and his deliverance has come through the death and resurrection of the Lord Jesus Christ.

In light of all this, we should do three things. First, we should *remember God's deliverance in the past* and give thanks for Jesus! The cross of Jesus Christ is *the* event in history that we look back to, where God dealt with our sin once and for all and secured our deliverance for all eternity. Yes, the battle with sin is still very real, but the penalty for those sins has been dealt with once and for all by the cross of Christ.

Second, on the basis of that deliverance, we should *pray for God's deliverance in the present*—knowing that his mercy never fails, and we can put our trust in him. Sometimes he will answer that prayer by changing our circumstances for the better, but he does not promise that that will *always* be the case. Some people have trials that they will have to endure for the rest of their lives here on earth. It is only in the new creation that we will be free from all our suffering. But by dealing with the greatest problem of all, our sin, we know that our future is secure, and we will one day enjoy eternity in his presence.

Finally, we can join with David and countless other believers, and *praise the God who delivers us*, because we, too, have been given a new song to sing. It is a song that focuses on the Lord's kindness and goodness to us in Christ. And while we sing that song, may we also affirm our faith in him, dedicate our lives to him, and then proclaim his good news to others. This is not just David's God and Israel's God; *this is our God!* He is the God who comes and delivers, and he's given us a new song to sing.

But what does this all mean for Emily, for Joan, and for Kate? Their individual circumstances are very different, but they too need to remember God's deliverance in the past and then cry out for God's deliverance in the present. God has already shown them how much he loves them by sending Jesus to die for them; he lifted them out of the miry pit before, and on the basis of that deliverance, they can be confident that he will lift them out of the miry pit again.

Emily needs to repent of her adultery and end the affair with Jack. The Lord has humbled her and shown her the depths of her rebellion and sin, but she is not beyond the reach of his grace. His mercy toward her never fails. She needs to trust that even if she never marries, she has all she needs in Christ. And when being single is really tough, she needs to cry out to him.

Joan needs to confess her bitterness of heart and learn to trust the Lord in her old age. Every stage of life brings new challenges, and not all of the trials we face will be sorted out in the here and now. She has lost sight of the Lord Jesus—

who loves her and has rescued her—and she needs to trust and depend on him all over again. Her body will continue to deteriorate, and it will one day fail, but because of his death and resurrection she doesn't need to fear the future. Because of his death and resurrection we can be confident that the Lord is able to bring us through death to eternal life. We can know that those who put their trust in him will live again and be in his presence forever.

And what about Kate? She needs to confess her coldness of heart and pray for her faith to be renewed and restored. She's become so preoccupied with running her children around that she has lost sight of where she really belongs and to whom she really belongs. Ballet dancing, playing the trumpet, and being on the soccer team are all good gifts from the Lord, but they will not last, and her children need to know that. She has the responsibility of preparing them for heaven—which is their real home and where they truly belong.

And what about you? I don't know the situations you are facing, but my guess is there will be some reading this who are compromised and ensnared in sin, others who are consumed by bitterness and self-absorption, and still others who are preoccupied with the things of this world and coldhearted toward the Lord. Will you hear the voice of the Lord as he speaks to you in the words of this psalm? Will you give thanks that God's deliverance has come in the Lord Jesus Christ? And on the basis of that deliverance in the past, will you pray for his deliverance in the present?

There may be some reading this who know they are unable to do this because they have no knowledge of the Lord's deliverance in the past. You may have been part of a church family for many years but have never cried out to the Lord and have no personal experience of his forgiveness and deliverance. Or maybe you are very new to all of this and have been persuaded by a friend to read this book—but you can hear the Lord speaking to you through his Word. What do you need to do? You need to admit your need, believe in what the Lord Jesus has done for you on the cross, and then cry out to him for deliverance. Let him lift you out of the miry swamp and put your feet on solid ground. And then join with the rest of us as we sing that new song in our hearts—a song of praise to the God who comes and delivers.

REFLECTION AND DISCUSSION QUESTIONS

1) Psalm 40 presents in a unique way God's spectacular showing of himself. In what way(s) does God reveal himself, and what aspects of God do we glimpse through these words of David?

2) Before bringing New Testament light to this psalm, Carrie Sandom reads it in its original context, as David's own testimony to God's deliverance. How does the psalm's text show David's aim not only to praise the Lord personally but also to share that praise with others?

3) This psalm is meant to stretch our thoughts all the way to Christ our Savior. In what ways do Luke 24:44–45 and Hebrews 10:4–7 help make the connections?

4) As God shows himself to us in all these passages so far (Exodus 19; 1 Kings 8; Isaiah 6; and Psalm 40), what common words and themes do you find? Why do we keep finding these?

5) In what ways might you have experienced or witnessed real-life challenges similar to those offered as examples by Carrie Sandom? How does an encounter with the God of Psalm 40 shed light on those challenges?

5

On Another Mountain

THE GOD WHO POINTS TO HIS SON

Matthew 17:1–15

NANCY LEIGH DEMOSS

What took place on the Mount of Transfiguration may be the most important event between Jesus's birth and his death and resurrection. The more I linger in this account, the greater the challenge to deal with it in one message. In fact, one pastor I know recently preached some dozen sermons on Mark's record of the transfiguration. Not to worry . . . we'll keep it to one!

One of the first things that strikes me about this event is the number of different voices speaking. What a tragedy it would have been if the disciples had walked away from this mountaintop experience focusing on Peter's voice, or on the words of Moses and Elijah, rather than on that ringing declaration of the Father from the cloud, shining the spotlight on his Son. "Listen to *him*," the Father said. As we meditate on this passage, my prayer is that our attention will be directed to Jesus and that we will all listen to *him*.

We have been considering a progression of passages in which God reveals himself in spectacular ways. In the passage before us, God manifests himself through the glory of his Son. May the Spirit grant us eyes to see, ears to hear, and hearts to receive all that he has for us as we together focus on Jesus.

The account of the transfiguration is recorded in all three Synoptic Gospels. As is generally the case in Scripture, this passage takes on greater meaning when it is understood in the context of what precedes and follows it. The same sequence can be seen in Matthew's, Mark's, and Luke's Gospels. In Matthew's case, the stage for the transfiguration (chapter 17) is set in chapter 16. Jesus wants his disciples to understand who he is—his *identity*. And so he inquires of them, "Who do people say that the Son of Man is?" (16:13).

As is true today, there was a great deal of confusion and a variety of opinions concerning the question of Jesus's identity. But the general consensus as reported by the disciples was that Jesus was a great prophet who had risen from the dead— a great man on a level with John the Baptist or perhaps with Old Testament prophets such as Elijah or Jeremiah. It is clear that people thought highly of Jesus. Yet they still considered him one among many.

Jesus's next question for the disciples is one we all must answer: "But who do you say that I am?" (v. 15). It is this question that brings forth Peter's bold profession that Jesus is not one among many. Rather, he is the one and only—the Messiah—the anointed one: "You are the Christ, the Son of the living God" (v. 16). Peter gets it, at least at that moment—the glorious truth of the deity of Christ. *The reason Peter gets it is the same reason any of us gets any spiritual truth: it has been revealed to him by the Father* (v. 17).

On the heels of Peter's great profession comes the first mention in Matthew's Gospel of the church. The truth of who Jesus is leads to the promise that he will build and preserve his church (v. 18). He speaks of the keys of the kingdom of heaven (v. 19). Jesus then commands the disciples to keep this good news to themselves—not to tell anyone that he is the Christ (v. 20). The Jewish expectations of the Messiah did not have room for the Messiah to suffer and die. Jesus didn't want anyone or anything to deter him from that objective—the very purpose for which he was sent to earth.

The next verse (v. 21) is a pivotal point in the Gospel narrative. The course of Jesus's ministry now turns explicitly, intentionally toward the cross. He begins to explain to his disciples what lies ahead. What we see unfolding through these next chapters is the theme of *humiliation* and *exaltation*—first suffering and then glory. First the cross and then the crown.

In verse 21 we have Jesus's first recorded prediction of his death: "From that time Jesus began to show his disciples that he must go to Jerusalem and suffer many things from the elders and chief priests and scribes, and be killed." First comes humiliation—suffering and death. The verse continues: ". . . and on the third day be raised." After humiliation—exaltation.

But Peter, speaking for the rest of the disciples, does not understand such talk. It makes no sense at all to him because his theology, like that of other Jews, has no place for a Messiah who suffers and dies. The Jews were looking for a powerful king! Peter actually rebukes Jesus, as if to say, "No way! This will never happen to you!" (see v. 22).

Jesus's words about the resurrection clearly have not registered; instead, Peter gets stuck on the part about suffering and dying. *He is suffering-averse. He wants exaltation without humiliation. He wants glory without suffering. He wants a crown without a cross. And don't we often want the same thing?*

In response, Jesus strongly reprimands Peter, telling him: "You are thinking man's way, not God's way" (see v. 23). You see, God's kingdom advances not only *in spite of* suffering and humiliation. As the theology of suffering is developed through the Scriptures, we realize that God's kingdom advances *by means of suffering, humiliation, and weakness. In the inscrutable wisdom of God, death brings life.*

In the closing paragraph of Matthew 16, leading right up to the Mount of Transfiguration, Jesus explains to his disciples that not only must *he* suffer (a concept already incomprehensible to them), but also *they* must suffer: "If anyone would come after me, let him deny himself and take up his cross and follow me" (v. 24). Jesus is saying, in effect, "If you want to share in my kingdom, if you want to share in my exaltation, you have to take the pathway of the cross. There's no way around it."

However, Jesus reminds his disciples that the pathway does not end at the cross. If humiliation—suffering—were all we had to expect or anticipate, our lives would be dismal and pointless. We would live in perpetual discouragement. In the chapter's final two verses, Jesus spells out the certain hope that humiliation will be followed by exaltation. Suffering will be followed by glory.

It's true of Christ. And it's true of his followers. "For the Son of Man is going to come with his angels in the glory of his Father, and then he will repay [or *reward*, some translations say] each person according to what he has done" (v. 27). When he appears in glory at the end of this age, he will reward his faithful followers, and he will punish his enemies. The message is clear: first comes humiliation and then will come glorious exaltation. First suffering, then glory.

The promise of ultimate glory in verse 27 is linked to a more immediate promise of glory in verse 28: "Truly, I say to you," Jesus says, "there are some standing here who will not taste death until they see the Son of Man coming in his kingdom." This promise is fulfilled in the next paragraph (the opening of Matthew 17) as a few select disciples are given a preview of Christ's coming in power and glory to set up his kingdom—that moment when he will return in all his glory to judge the wicked and to reign forever with his saints.

The *transfiguration is an unveiling of the glory of the King*. From his birth until this moment Jesus has been clothed in the humble garb of humanity. But now these few disciples are going to get a glimpse of the royal robes of his deity. They're going to see his glory.

THE KING'S GLORY UNVEILED

In this context, then, we arrive at Matthew 17:1, on the alert for glory. "And after six days Jesus took with him Peter and James, and John his brother, and led them up a high mountain by themselves." Luke's Gospel tells us that Jesus took these disciples with him up on the mountain *to pray* (9:28). I don't think it is insignificant that Jesus's transfiguration took place as he was praying, seeking his Father's face. We're also reminded that *the most intimate experiences of God's glory rarely take place in a crowd.* We have to be willing to pull away—to leave the rush of the crowd and to spend time in his presence.

These same three disciples were soon to witness Jesus's humiliation—his agony in Gethsemane, and finally his death on the cross. Surely the experience of seeing his glory on the mountain helped prepare them to see his suffering in the days that were to follow. And entering into his passion helped prepare them for their future ministry, for the suffering they would be called to endure in the birthing and nurturing of the church.

Think about it. Had they just experienced the sufferings of Gethsemane and the cross without seeing the glory of the transfiguration, they likely would have felt disillusioned, discouraged, and hopeless. On the other hand, had they only experienced the exaltation of the transfiguration without witnessing the humiliation of Christ's passion, they easily could have become unduly elated, as Paul talks about in 2 Corinthians 12. Their expectations of what it meant to be a follower of Christ would have been unrealistic.

First humiliation, then exaltation. *Through the course of the Christian life, there will be seasons of glory and seasons of gore. Our souls will be strengthened as we remember that Christ has been through both and that he goes with us through both of those seasons.*

Now note that this experience takes place on a "high mountain" (Matt. 17:1). This is not the first time the presence of God has been revealed on a mountain. It was on Mount Moriah that God provided for Abraham and Isaac a sacrifice, pointing us to the sacrifice of himself yet to come. It was on Mount Sinai that God revealed himself to Moses and the children of Israel, giving them his law. On both Mount Sinai and the Mount of Transfiguration, God allowed his glory to blaze forth for his people to see. On all three mountains, God spoke. But on this mountain, God's glory is displayed through his final, perfect Word—his Son.

Matthew 17:2 takes us right into the main event on this high mountain: "He was transfigured before them." *Transfigured* comes from the Greek word from which we get our English word *metamorphosis*. It means "changed in form"—transformed. "He was transfigured before them, and his face shone like the sun, and his clothes became white as light." This whole experience is a vivid confirmation of the confession just made by Peter: this is indeed "the Christ, the Son of the living God."

This event appears to have taken place at night. Jesus was transfigured from the inside out as the glory and splendor of God became visible and shone forth. "His face shone like the sun"—picture the sun bursting out in brilliance from behind dark clouds, as its dazzling splendor suddenly confronts us, warms us, almost blinds us. It was like that, only surely much more glorious.

And then there was the matter of his clothing. When Moses's face shone with the glory of God, he covered it up with a veil. But Jesus's glory, the glory of his God-ness, his God-hood, his deity, was so bright that his clothes shone, too, becoming white as light. The other Gospel writers tell us that his clothing became "dazzling white" (Luke 9:29), that his clothes were "radiant, intensely white, as no one on earth could bleach them" (Mark 9:3).

As we meditate on this picture of blazing, blinding light from Jesus's face and from the dazzling whiteness of his clothes, we should not imagine that it was as if a bright spotlight shone upon Jesus. *Rather, this was the manifestation of the glory of God from within.* Up to this moment, while he was here on earth, Christ's glory had been veiled by his humanity, his body of flesh. But now, for a moment, the veil was lifted and his glory was made visible to human eyes—"the glory of God revealed in the face of Jesus Christ," as Paul says in 2 Corinthians 4:6. One commentator says, "Essentially, this was not a new miracle, but the temporary cessation of an ongoing miracle. The real miracle was that Jesus most of the time could keep from displaying this glory."[1]

This was the occasion during Jesus's earthly life that the fullness of the Godhead shone most clearly and brilliantly through the veil of his humanity. There on the mountain, the three disciples were given a glimpse of the glory that Jesus had had for all eternity past.

Some thirty years later, Peter was still so taken by this event that he referred to it in his second epistle: "We were eyewitnesses of his majesty. . . . We were with him on the holy mountain" (2 Pet. 1:16, 18).

The glory that was manifested on the Mount of Transfiguration is the glory of the Word, who was with God, and was God, from the beginning, the Word made flesh so that "we have seen his glory, glory as of the only Son from the Father, full of grace and truth" (John 1:1–2, 14). This is the glory we saw on Mount Sinai, with all its thunder and lightning and

---

[1] David Guzik, *Commentary on the Bible*, http://www.studylight.org/com/guz/view.cgi?book=mt&chapter=17&verse=1#Mt17_1.

trumpet blasts, so that the people trembled (Ex. 19:16). This is the glory we saw in 1 Kings 8—the glory that so filled the house of the Lord that the priests could not even stand up to minister (vv. 10–11). This is the glory Isaiah saw high and lifted up, whose voice made the foundations of the thresholds shake and the temple fill with smoke (Isa. 6:1–4). This is that same glory of the same God. His glory stretches into eternity past, and it will shine forth into eternity future.

In this sacred moment on the mount, *the disciples were given a preview of Christ's future return in power and in glory—a foretaste of the day when his full glory will be eternally unveiled.* His messianic kingdom will be established on this earth, not in humiliation but in exaltation—the Lion of the tribe of Judah on the throne forever and ever. When we come to the book of Revelation, we read about this same glorious Lord, who appears to John with a face "like the sun shining in full strength" (Rev. 1:16). This is the one before whom myriads of myriads and thousands of thousands cry out with a loud voice, "Worthy is the Lamb who was slain, to receive power and wealth and wisdom and might and honor and glory and blessing!" (Rev. 5:11–12).

THE ULTIMATE EXODUS

At this point, there on the Mount of Transfiguration, Matthew's "And behold" in 17:3 alerts us to the sudden appearance of Moses and Elijah, talking with Jesus. These are glorified saints. Moses had been dead for about fourteen hundred years, and Elijah had been taken in a chariot of fire a little more than nine hundred years earlier. Yet both are still alive—a reminder of the immortality of the soul and the conscious existence of human beings after this life, including our loved ones who have died in Christ and are still very much alive today.

Why Moses and Elijah, specifically? Their appearance may represent several things, most clearly the Old Testament Law and the Prophets, all of which pointed forward to Jesus the Messiah who has now come and fulfilled their words. Together with the disciples, they may also represent a picture of all those who will be with Christ in his coming kingdom, both Old Testament saints and New Testament saints. Moses may be a type of those who have died and will be raised when Christ returns and Elijah a type of those who will be still alive and caught up to meet the Lord in the air.

Wouldn't you love to have heard this conversation among Moses, Elijah, and Jesus? What do you suppose they talked about? Luke lets us in on at least some of the exchange: "[They] spoke of his *departure*, which he was about to accomplish at Jerusalem" (9:31). Your translation may read, "his *decease.*" The word here literally means "exodus." They spoke of his exodus, his exit, his *death*. In 2 Peter 1:15, the apostle uses the same term to speak of his own imminent death.

Consider for a moment this word *exodus*. Nearly fifteen hundred years earlier, when the children of Israel were slaves in Egypt, in bondage to cruel taskmasters, God had raised up a deliverer named Moses. Moses had led the children of Israel out of Egypt in what became known as "the exodus." Now, here is this same deliverer talking with Jesus, the great deliverer, about Jesus's coming exodus—his death, followed by his resurrection and his ascension to heaven.

How Moses must have rejoiced to see the arrival of the ultimate exodus, the one toward which his exodus centuries earlier had pointed. Finally the time had come for the exodus through which God would bring deliverance to Adam's helpless race, so long enslaved to sin.

I wonder what these Old Testament saints said about Christ's death. Did they discuss how the prophets had foretold his suffering and sacrificial death? Did they talk about why he was going to die? Did Jesus explain what his death would accomplish for the redemption of the souls of men? All the possibilities point us to the cross, the watershed moment of all of human history—the humiliation and the suffering that would precede Christ's ultimate exaltation and glory. At the heart of this scene of glory is the central fact that Jesus is heading straight to the cross.

Now, parenthetically, at this point in the narrative, Luke includes a detail that is not reported in the other Gospels: "Peter and those who were with him were heavy with sleep, but when they became fully awake they saw his glory and the two men who stood with him" (9:32). Apparently, Moses and Elijah made their appearance while the disciples were dozing. These same disciples, you may recall, would also sleep through Jesus's agony in Gethsemane. How in the world could they sleep then? And how could they sleep at a time like this?

Maybe an even more important question for us is how can *we* sleep when Christ is displaying his glory around us? It makes me want to pray, "Lord, awaken us to see your glory!"

Finally awake and alert, Peter speaks up by stating the obvious: "It is good that we are here" (Matt. 17:4). Yes, that was certainly true.

All three Gospels record the infamous suggestion with which Peter follows up this comment. As Matthew records it, Peter says to Jesus, "If you wish, I will make three tents [or shelters or tabernacles] here, one for you and one for Moses and one for Elijah" (v. 4).

You've perhaps had the discussion with friends over a meal: "If you could invite three people who've ever lived as guests to dinner, whom would you invite and why?" Well, this has to be it for Peter: Jesus, Moses, and Elijah—it doesn't get much better than that! But now two of the guests are leaving. Peter somehow realizes this scene is hugely significant. He knows he is watching history in the making, and he wants to capture the moment, to bottle the experience, to retain the glow.

But has Peter forgotten what Jesus had just told them about his death? Is he trying to keep that from happening? Is he trying to avoid the cross? Yes, it is good to be there; but they are not intended to *stay* there—not yet.

During this conference, we experienced sweet moments of fellowship, worship, and blessing, accompanied by a special sense of the presence of Christ. To some extent, at least, we left our problems behind. We were able to put our pressures and problems on "pause." We thought, *Wow, it's great to be here. Wouldn't it be wonderful if we could just camp out here for a while! Who wants to leave what we've got here—especially if we're going back to a stress-filled set of circumstances?*

These disciples, with their spokesman Peter, preferred to stay right where they were, up on the mountain in company with these three great men, rather than join the multitude down in the valley below, where there was misery and unbelief, where there would be a confrontation with the desperate father of a demonized son, in the very next verses.

They would surely rather stay on the mountain than go on to Jerusalem, where Jesus was to suffer and die. Who wouldn't? It was this same desire to avoid suffering that was evidenced in Peter's rebuke to Jesus in the previous chapter, when Jesus spoke of his suffering and death.

Peter speaks for all of us who long to experience glory without suffering, exaltation without humiliation. But we cannot have one without the other. The way of glory is the way of the cross. Jesus came not for the building of any new tent or tabernacle but rather to tabernacle with us in his very flesh, which would be struck down and then raised three days later. Peter did not grasp this truth at that point; in fact, Luke tells us Peter didn't know what he was saying (Luke 9:33). So often, we don't either. Peter's timing was off. God's plan was the cross, which, thank God, Jesus gladly chose to embrace, rather than to stay there on the mountain where he was.

LISTEN TO JESUS!

Matthew 17:5 tells us that Peter "was still speaking when, behold, a bright cloud overshadowed them, and a voice from the cloud said, 'This is my beloved Son, with whom I am well pleased.'" The Father had made the same affirmation some three years earlier, at Jesus's baptism (3:17).

As we've been reminded, in the Old Testament a cloud was often a visible symbol of God's presence. When the law was given at Mount Sinai, God came in a thick, dark cloud, with thunder and lightning, and the whole mountain was wrapped in smoke as the Lord descended in fire (Ex. 19:9, 16–18). At the dedication of Solomon's temple, the cloud of God's presence coming into the house of the Lord was so great the priests could not stand to minister (1 Kings 8:10–11). Our holy God is a righteous judge whose presence is threatening to sinful man.

But here on the Mount of Transfiguration the cloud that overshadows them is "bright" (Matt. 17:5)—perhaps a hint that at this moment in human history God's mercy and grace are being revealed and all his redemptive promises are being fulfilled through his Son, who will satisfy the Father's righteous wrath by offering up himself as a substitute for guilty sinners.

Keep in mind that the transfiguration was intended to reveal Jesus's identity to his disciples. Jesus's question to Peter in the previous chapter, and Peter's great confession, reach into this scene for the full, shining answer. While Peter is still speaking, the Father interrupts to make it clear that Jesus is not merely one of three great men. Jesus and Moses and Elijah are not equals, not even close. Jesus is the one and only, the incomparable Christ. Moses and Elijah were servants in God's house. But Jesus is the Son, the beloved Son, "with whom [his Father is] well pleased."

God has always been pleased with his Son. Through all of eternity in heaven and then through his years on earth, the Son never for a single moment displeased the Father. God was pleased with the sacrifice Jesus was about to offer for the sins of mankind, the sacrifice of his life.

God says of his Son, "Listen to him" (v. 5). He is telling the disciples, in effect, "It's better to hear Jesus than to see Moses and Elijah back from the dead." Yes, throughout the Old Testament, God had spoken through his prophets, but again and again the people had refused to listen to the prophets; in so doing, they had refused to listen to the voice of God.

Now, in these latter days, God has done what he promised to do back in Deuteronomy 18:15, where Moses said: "The LORD your God will raise up for you a prophet like me from among you. . . . It is to him you shall listen." God sent his only begotten Son and said, "Listen to him." For when Jesus speaks, God speaks. And as we read the written Word of God, we are listening to Jesus.

Peter and the other disciples needed this admonition in their day, and we as believers need the same exhortation in our day: *Listen to him.*

- When you don't know what to say or do, don't talk; *listen to Jesus.*
- When you're confused and don't know what to believe, *listen to Jesus.*
- When God's ways are contrary to your natural ways of thinking, don't trust your own heart; *listen to Jesus.*
- When you're surrounded by great Bible teachers and preachers, respected authors and spiritual leaders, don't make idols of them; *listen to Jesus.*
- When you're tempted, as Peter was, to give God direction, *listen to Jesus.*
- And when you think you know what to do next ("Let's build three tents here"), put away your foolish plans, and *listen to Jesus.*

"When the disciples heard this," Matthew tells us, "they fell on their faces and were terrified. But Jesus came and touched them, saying, 'Rise, and have no fear.' And when they lifted up their eyes, they saw no one but Jesus only" (17:6–8). I find it interesting that no one fell on his face when Peter spoke, and no one fell on his face when Moses and Elijah spoke. It makes me wonder if one of the reasons people aren't falling on their faces in our churches today may be that we're not listening to God.

When they hear the voice of God, they fall on their faces, terrified. It's an experience that Isaiah had, that Ezekiel had, that Daniel had; it's an experience that the apostle John had in the book of Revelation. These men were overcome by the voice of God—a reminder of the awesome power of God's Word.

Mercifully, in spite of their terror, the disciples are not consumed by the glory of God. We see the mercy of Christ when he touches them and says, "'Rise, and have no fear.' And when they lifted up their eyes, they saw no one but Jesus only" (vv. 7–8). I love that. Isn't that what we need today? To see Jesus only, to have his presence eclipse every other reality, blessing, and concern?

Moses and Elijah are no longer needed; their role is finished. The disciples are now left alone with Christ. His coming work at the cross would be sufficient, as Christ alone would fulfill God's redemptive plan. Moses and Elijah—great men of God—are now gone, but Christ is still with them. And when the spiritual giants who have made a mark on your life disappear from your sight and are nowhere to be found in your circumstances, remember that Christ is still with you. He is fully able to meet every need, now and always.

"And as they were coming down the mountain, Jesus commanded them, 'Tell no one the vision, until the Son of Man is raised from the dead'" (v. 9). This echoes his similar warning in the previous chapter (16:20). Jesus knew that some would want to take him and make him king before his death and resurrection. But he was headed to the cross. He understood what the disciples didn't: that John the Baptist had already fulfilled the prophecy of Elijah's coming, and that John the Baptist's suffering paved the way for the suffering of the Christ (Matt. 17:10–13). Jesus is embracing his imminent suffering.

As Jesus comes down from that Mount of Transfiguration, we see his willing—and costly—submission to the will of his Father. We've seen a glimpse of what he laid aside to come to this earth—the glory that was his from all eternity. From a human perspective, I believe Jesus could have gone back to heaven in that moment. There was the thinnest of veils between him and heaven at that point. He could have, on a human level, avoided the cross. But he chose to go back down the mountain, to deal with human need, demonic forces, sickness, sin, and death. He chose the humiliation and agony of the cross, for us.

HIS TRANSFORMATION AND OURS

So what bearing does this magnificent account have on our lives today? Two personal implications (among many possible ones) have been on my heart as I've been meditating on this passage.

First, *for those who are in Christ, his transfiguration points to our transformation.* The purpose of his death and his resurrection (i.e., what he was talking about up there on the mountain— his *exodus* from this life) was to rescue us from sin and death, to redeem and make all things new by means of his death on our behalf and his resurrection.

Christ's transfiguration points to our transformation in a past, present, and future sense. For starters, those of us who are in Christ have been made a new creation. It's past. It's done. According to 2 Corinthians 5:17, "The old has passed away; behold, the new has come." Our sins have been forgiven through the blood of Christ, and our spirits have been made alive by his Spirit. We know this as *justification*—the transformation from death to life, from darkness to light, from being outside of Christ to being in Christ. Christians have been justified, made a new creation, in Christ.

For those who have been justified (past tense), a present transformation is taking place as we are gradually being changed into the image of Christ, and his nature is increasingly manifest in us. We call this *sanctification*—the process by which we are transformed into his likeness, by his indwelling presence. His transfiguration on the mount gives us this hope.

This word, *transfigured*, is used in only two other places in the New Testament apart from the Gospel accounts. They shed light on this present transformation. First, in Romans 12:2 Paul exhorts: "Do not be conformed to this world, but be *transformed* [*transfigured, metamorphosed*] by the renewal of your mind." Then, in 2 Corinthians 3:18, the process of our transformation is described: "And we all, with unveiled face, beholding the glory of the Lord, are being *transformed* into the same image from one degree of glory to another. For this comes from the Lord who is the Spirit."

These verses help us understand sanctification as that process of transformation that the Spirit of Christ brings about in believers during our lives here on earth, in preparation for eternity in heaven. This process takes place as we fix our eyes on Christ, "beholding [his] glory." The psalmist expressed the same heart:

One thing have I asked of the LORD,
    that will I seek after:
that I may dwell in the house of the LORD
    all the days of my life,
to gaze upon the beauty of the LORD
    and to inquire in his temple. (Ps. 27:4)

It's as we gaze steadfastly upon Christ that we are transfigured into his likeness. There is no other way.

Do you want to be like Jesus? Do you want his glory to be increasingly manifest in and through your life? It will happen as you spend time in his presence beholding him.

When speaking on the topic of cultivating intimacy with God through the practice of a daily devotional life, I often ask the women attending to be honest enough to raise their hand if at this point in time they do not have a consistent devotional habit. Invariably the response is the same, whether the question is asked of young women, older women, Bible study leaders, pastors' wives, people in vocational ministry—all kinds of women. Approximately 90 percent say, "I don't currently have a consistent devotional life." I mention this not to create guilt but to stress that there is no shortcut to spiritual transformation, hard as we might try to find one.

It is through beholding Christ in his Word that we see him and are transformed into his image, "from one degree of glory to another" (2 Cor. 3:18). I thank God for the blessing and influence of godly preachers and good books. But they are only useful to the extent that they help us get to Jesus. They are no substitute for spending time with Christ himself. They cannot transform us. Only Jesus can do that.

So there's past transformation, as we have been made new creatures in Christ through justification. And there's present, ongoing transformation, the sanctification that is taking place in our lives as we behold Christ. And finally there is future transformation—the glorification to which we look forward with great anticipation.

The transfiguration of Christ gives us a preview of what God has in store for us as one day we will be perfect in body, soul, and spirit, perfectly reflecting our now risen Lord. Not only will we be finally without sin but also our physical bodies will be transformed and perfected—all because of what Christ accomplished for us by his *exodus*, his death, resurrection, and ascension. As Paul says in Philippians 3:20–21: "Our citizenship is in heaven, and from it we await a Savior, the Lord Jesus Christ, who will transform our lowly body [humiliation] to be like his glorious body [exaltation]."

I can hardly wait! I long for that day. I long for it even more because of what I've seen in the transfiguration of Christ. When Christ returns, we will be finally changed, from the inside out. Everything about us, including our bodies, will be redeemed and restored. That which is now lowly will be glorious. This transformation is beginning in us now, as we are becoming like Jesus, and when he returns, it will finally be complete. We will be glorified.

The Scriptures paint a vision of this transformation—this transfiguration—in verses like these:

The path of the righteous is like the light of dawn, which shines brighter and brighter until full day. (Prov. 4:18)

Those who are wise shall shine like the brightness of the
sky above, and those who turn many to righteousness, like
the stars forever and ever. (Dan. 12:3)

Let those who love him be like the rising of the sun in its
might. (Judg. 5:31 NASB)

And what's the point of it all? To have people say how magnificent we are? No! It's to have people look at us and say,
"How glorious is Christ!" Like the moon, we have no light of
our own. We are simply reflectors of Christ in us, the hope of
glory. It's his light that we are to manifest, his glory that we
want seen, felt, and known through us in this world.

The first personal implication, then, is that for those who
are in Christ, his transfiguration points to our transformation.

HOPE FOR LIFE IN THE VALLEY

The second implication is that *Christ's transfiguration on the
mountain gives us context, perspective, and hope for life in the valley.*

It was the vision of Christ's glory on the mount that prepared the disciples for what lay ahead after they came down.
And what we see of Jesus on the mount (and throughout the
Scriptures) should prepare us for whatever we may face as we
labor for his kingdom and await his return in glory.

We have seen the theme of humiliation that leads to exaltation. We have seen Jesus aiming for the cross, even in this
passage where he is crowned with heavenly glory. Christ's
transfiguration on the mountain gives us hope as we walk
with him down into the valley full of troubles and ultimately
to the cross. As Paul explains in 2 Corinthians 4:17, our "light

momentary affliction is preparing for us an eternal weight of glory beyond all comparison."

Thank God for those moments when we are permitted a glimpse of the splendor and the glory of Christ. But those moments "on the mount" simply don't happen every day, and they generally don't last long. The disciples had to come down from the mountain, and so must we. Glimpses like the one in this scene of transfiguration are simply a foretaste, intended to make us long for the eternal glory and to help us endure the suffering down in the valley. The suffering sometimes feels eternal, but weighty and interminable as it may seem, God's Word reminds us that our suffering in this life is "light momentary affliction"—in light of the glory that awaits us. And we have seen that glory in Christ.

In Matthew 17:9 we see Jesus and his disciples coming down the mountain. As they talk, and as Jesus explains the role of the prophets Elijah and John the Baptist who heralded his coming, Jesus again clearly predicts his suffering. Just as John the Baptist was rejected and killed by the leaders, "so also the Son of Man will certainly suffer at their hands" (v. 12). This is the one who has just been revealed in his glory as the Son of God. But this *Son of Man*, he reminds them, must suffer and die. Humiliation will precede his final, eternal exaltation. And his followers should expect the same.

The scene they encounter when they finally reach the valley below is a far cry from what they have just experienced up on the mountain. Down in the valley, they are immediately confronted with a chaotic crowd of onlookers; a desperate man begging for mercy for his son; a demon-possessed epileptic who "suffers terribly," falling into the fire and water; and a band of disciples who are helpless to deal with the whole situation. There's consternation down in the valley; there's confusion; there's a morass of human need.

Where do we live most of our lives in this world? Not up on the mountain where we have a stunning vision of glory but down in the valley below, where we must walk by faith in what we cannot see. Down in the valley, where we are faced with suffering we can't handle and expectations we can't possibly meet. How often do people bring tough situations to us, hoping that we can do something about them? People come to us and plead: "My husband . . . my kids . . . my job . . . my church . . . What can you do to help?" How often do we face such situations ourselves?

Here's the point: the Christ who manifested his glory on the mount went with his disciples down into the valley where the glory was once again veiled. And that same Christ will go with you into every valley.

I'm confident that Peter and James and John never, ever forgot what they had heard and seen on the mount, even though for a while they couldn't talk about it to anybody else. They were meant to see the circumstances down in the valley in light of the glory of Christ that they had witnessed up on the mount. The God of glory is the God of all grace, and the God who spoke and manifested his greatness up on the mountain is the same God who speaks and exercises his power over evil in the valley, even now.

In his name, evil flees, just as that demon fled from the man's son at Jesus's rebuke. The God of glory is the God who sent his beloved Son to die on the cross for us so that sin and death could finally be conquered and eternal glory be the crown of all those who belong to Christ.

In the meantime, we walk through valleys. But the account of Christ's transfiguration gives us perspective and hope as we experience life on this prodigal planet.

BEHOLDING HIM

As I have pondered the account of the transfiguration, I'll confess that at times this picture of glory has seemed far and disconnected from the reality of my own life and pain. I have grappled to discover what meaningful bearing this passage has on a number of challenging situations I have faced in recent months.

And I know I'm not alone. There are many moms and grandmoms reading this who cry themselves to sleep at night over a prodigal son or daughter or grandchild. You may be facing intense financial hardship. Or perhaps you're a widow dealing with the recent loss of a mate. Maybe you have a chronic, debilitating health issue, or you're in the thick of a church conflict that is about to explode, or you're struggling to keep your equilibrium in a frayed marriage.

You may feel like your life is imploding, as I have sometimes felt when pressed by painful, inexplicable circumstances. And perhaps, to you, this account and others we've been looking at seem far removed from the reality of your life.

Please hear me when I say that the theme of this conference, "Here Is Our God," is exactly what I need—right here and now, in the midst of my valley. And it is exactly what you need in your life circumstances, however difficult or harrowing they may be.

The glorious, all-powerful, resurrected, ascended, reigning Christ has given us his Spirit, and he goes with us down into the valley and the challenges of life in this fallen world. Right there, in the valley, he gives us hope. He gives us perspective. He gives us strength. He gives us courage. He gives us grace.

And he uses all those issues as a means to transform us. Our hope is not just that we'll finally make it to heaven having merely survived earth's messy problems but that we will *thrive* as we are sustained by his presence and power. And as we walk through the valley, we cling—sometimes with raw, naked faith—to the hope that in God's sovereign wisdom, the humility and suffering of this season will one day be replaced by unending exaltation and glory.

In that brief span between the glory that Jesus had in eternity past and the glory that will be his for all eternity to come, Jesus took on human flesh. His glory was veiled as he suffered for us. And because of what he has done for us on the cross, because of his *exodus*, our span of suffering in these bodies of flesh in this broken world will soon give way to eternal future glory with our glorified Lord. So take heart, my sisters, and be of courage, for he has promised:

> You make known to me the path of life;
>> in your presence there is fullness of joy;
>> at your right hand are pleasures forevermore.
>> (Ps. 16:11)

A few days ago, a friend, knowing the pain of my current valley, said to me, "How are you doing?" I said, by faith, what I know in my heart to be true: "All is well in heaven; and all will be well on earth." It's a certain hope, rooted in the real-

ity of the glorified Savior the disciples witnessed there on
the mount.

"Though you have not seen him," Peter later wrote, "you
love him. Though you do not now see him, you believe in
him and rejoice with joy that is inexpressible and filled with
glory, obtaining the outcome of your faith, the salvation of
your souls" (1 Pet. 1:8–9).

Peter never forgot the glory he had seen, the glory of
Christ, the Son of God. May we behold Christ through God's
Word, listen to him, believe, and rejoice with joy that is inexpressible and filled with glory. May we follow our Savior
in the way of the cross that leads to the crown. And may our
lives reflect in ever-increasing measure the glory of God the
Father, the Son, and the Holy Spirit. Amen.

REFLECTION AND DISCUSSION QUESTIONS

1) What details from Matthew 17:1–13 bring to mind details
   from the Old Testament passages we have seen (Exodus 19;
   1 Kings 8; Isaiah 6; Psalm 40)? What connections do you
   find among all these scenes?

2) In the paragraphs on either side of this scene in Matthew
   17, find Jesus's insistent focus on his suffering and death to
   come. Why this scene at this point? What does the context
   show us about the Lord Jesus?

3) Nancy Leigh DeMoss invites us to identify with Peter,
   James, and John in this scene. In what ways do you identify? How does this scene challenge you personally?

4) Peter comments specifically on the transfiguration in
   2 Peter 1:16–21. How does Peter's point in this passage

connect to his mountaintop experience with Jesus? How does Peter help us with our "take-away" from the Mount of Transfiguration?

5) On that mountain with Jesus, John also gained crucial background for his further prophetic ministry. What must it have been like to encounter the figure of the risen Christ (Rev. 1:12–19)? What difference will it make to you even this day, to have encountered in the Word the glorious truth of who Christ is?

6

In the Third Heaven

THE GOD WHO CAN'T BE TALKED ABOUT

2 Corinthians 12

JENNY SALT

At the risk of nurturing a gender stereotype, I have to admit that I have a terrible sense of direction. It doesn't seem to matter whether I am driving or walking, whether I am in the familiar territory of the city of Sydney or any other place in the world. I always feel that I know the right direction, and I so often end up going exactly the wrong way.

When I was living in Chicago a few years ago, I remember driving into the city from the northern suburbs, making my way on roads I wasn't familiar with. The GPS told me to turn left, but my gut feeling was that that was the wrong way! And so I disregarded the directions and went a different way, and guess what? I got lost! It was ridiculous: I didn't know the roads, I didn't have any maps, and I didn't have any perspective to make a right judgment. The GPS with all its inbuilt maps and satellite positioning did have the right perspective! I heard that familiar word in a very calm American accent: "recalculating"—and then that all-knowing voice guided me back on track.

When it comes to a sense of direction, when I go with my gut, I lose perspective because I don't have all knowledge. I don't have the big picture.

The same thing can happen when we stand at the metaphorical corner and look at life, and, more specifically, as we look at weakness and strength. If we look at weakness and strength through the lens of the world,[1] then we can so easily get it wrong.

But when we look at weakness and strength through the lens of the gospel, it corrects our focus. Starting with the good news of Jesus Christ's death on our behalf and his resurrection from the dead, we see weakness and strength in their proper context. And that is what Paul addresses in 2 Corinthians 12, as he writes about boasting. Paul writes a lot about boasting in his letters to the Corinthians.

I don't know what you think about when you hear the word "boasting." In Australia (and I suspect in most places), we don't take kindly to people who boast about themselves, and most Aussies would not want to be seen as boasters—not obvious boasters, anyway.

If we *were* to talk about ourselves, if we *were* going to boast, the approach would naturally be to boast about the things

---

[1] By "the world," I mean something along the lines of the apostle John's use in his Gospel, as defined by D. A. Carson: "The created order (especially of human beings and human affairs) in rebellion against its maker." *The Gospel according to John* (Grand Rapids, MI: Eerdmans, 1991), 123.

that are impressive. So if you're training for a half-marathon, of course you will tell people you are training for a half-marathon. If you have just cooked up a storm to rival any contestant on *MasterChef*, then of course you will drop that into the conversation.[2] That's what we tend to do, if we are going to boast.

The world says boast about the good stuff, the impressive stuff, but don't boast in weakness. Hide weakness. Cover it up. Make sure no one sees it. That's what we think.

The message of the gospel is saying something quite different. *So how does the gospel lens change our view of weakness and strength?* That's what we will be thinking about as we focus on 2 Corinthians 12:1–10.

CONTEXT FIRST

To know what's going on in this chapter, we need to see it in context so that we understand why Paul is writing about weakness this way.

Paul wrote this letter for a number of reasons: to prepare the Corinthian Christians for his farewell visit, to remind and encourage them in their collection of money for the Jerusalem church, and to address issues that had arisen due to the presence of the so-called super-apostles and their assault on Paul's character.[3]

The letter reveals a range of emotions. Sometimes we read of Paul's joy and pride in the Corinthians. For example, in 2 Corinthians 7:4 he tells them: "I have spoken to you with

---

[2] *MasterChef* is a very popular cooking show in Australia.
[3] Paul Barnett, *The Message of 2 Corinthians*, The Bible Speaks Today (Nottingham, UK: Inter-Varsity, 1999), 16.

great frankness; I take great pride in you. I am greatly encouraged; in all our troubles my joy knows no bounds."[4]

In other places, however, Paul writes as one who is deeply hurt because the Corinthians are withholding their affection from him (6:12). They were easily swayed into believing criticisms that Paul was worldly (1:17), cowardly (1:23), exploitative (7:2), weak in speech while forceful in writing (10:1), a fool (11:1), and lacking the credentials of an apostle in terms of signs and wonders (12:11–12).[5] Paul's correspondence to the Corinthians is intensely personal, expressing a range of emotions from pride to sorrow.

Moreover, Paul is writing to people he knows and loves, so the words of 2 Corinthians 11:28 seem to fit well the context of the Corinthian church in particular: "Besides everything else, I face daily the pressure of my concern for all the churches." He had been the one to tell them about Jesus Christ; he was their spiritual father. He loved them and longed for them to grow strong in the gospel, to know the ongoing grace and comfort of Christ, who had died for them, risen from the dead, and sent his Spirit to dwell in them to the end.

Because he cared so deeply about the Corinthians, Paul was concerned to defend his ministry among them through this letter. Such a defense was needed because many in Corinth were starting to doubt his credentials. This was due in part to some visitors who had come to Corinth and were exerting a huge influence among the believers there.

This is the group Paul ironically calls "super-apostles"

---

[4] Unless otherwise indicated, Scripture quotations in this chapter are taken from *The Holy Bible, New International Version*®, NIV®. Copyright © 1973, 1978, 1984, 2011 by Biblica, Inc.™ Used by permission. All rights reserved worldwide.
[5] Barnett, *Message of 2 Corinthians*, 14.

(v. 5). We can glean a number of details about them from the letter itself. For example, they were preachers who came into Corinth with letters of recommendation, like curricula vitae—designed to impress. Paul refers with rather biting wit to these letters in 2 Corinthians 3:1–2: "Are we beginning to commend ourselves again? Or do we need, like some people, letters of recommendation to you or from you?"

These super-apostles were men who boasted about their heritage. Paul briefly joins their game to show the foolishness of this kind of boasting: "Are they Hebrews? So am I. Are they Israelites? So am I. Are they Abraham's descendants? So am I. Are they servants of Christ? (I am out of my mind to talk like this)" (2 Cor. 11:22–23). In other words, they were highlighting their superiority by boasting of their heritage in the line of Abraham.

These men were also, in commending themselves for their excellent public speaking, having a go at Paul for his apparently less than polished speaking. Paul himself is not hesitant to repeat these insults: "For some say, 'His letters are weighty and forceful, but in person he is unimpressive and his speaking amounts to nothing'" (10:10).

Not just with their words but also with their actions, these boasters aimed to build themselves up. They charged money for their services and exploited the Corinthians. Paul charges these swindlers, and he charges the Corinthians for allowing their exploitation: "In fact, you even put up with anyone who enslaves you or exploits you or takes advantage of you or pushes himself forward or slaps you in the face" (11:20).

Paul was not afraid to call these men, the so-called super-apostles, what they really were: false apostles, deceitful workmen, servants of Satan himself (vv. 13–14). The net result of their presence in Corinth was that they were undermining Paul, and to dismiss Paul was to dismiss the gospel message that he brought. The Corinthians were, so to speak, "throwing the baby out with the bathwater." To throw out Paul was to throw out the gospel of Jesus Christ.

And so Paul wanted the Corinthian Christians to know that they were thinking in a worldly way, looking at the surface of things, the outward, what was immediately impressive. They had their eyes on the seen; they had taken their eyes off what is unseen but what is of far greater worth.

With this context in mind, we come to chapter 12, where we read part of Paul's defense of his ministry and of himself as an apostle. As he makes his defense, he answers the question, *How does the gospel lens change our view of weakness and strength?* This passage answers that question in two ways.

1) THE GOSPEL LENS TRANSFORMS OUR BOASTING (2 COR. 12:1–6)

"I must go on boasting," Paul says (2 Cor. 12:1). The apostle Paul did not stop boasting, but his boasting was transformed through Christ. The nature of the transformation is this: looking through the gospel lens stops our boasting about things that make us look great.

Now, we don't really like it when people boast. No one likes the person who says, "Hey, look: I just got an A+!" Of course, when we're the achievers we *do* want people to know, but nobody likes the boaster who comes right out and says it.

In the Greek culture of Paul's day, however, boasting *was* acceptable, even commended. It's what the super-apostles were all about, and it's what the Corinthians valued. "Talking yourself up" was good.

Paul's perspective on boasting is quite different; he shows us what "gospel boasting" is. When he writes, "I must *go on* boasting," his words point the reader back to the immediately preceding verses:

> If I must boast, I will boast of the things that show my weakness. The God and Father of the Lord Jesus, who is to be praised forever, knows that I am not lying. In Damascus the governor under King Aretas had the city of the Damascenes guarded in order to arrest me. But I was lowered in a basket from a window in the wall and slipped through his hands. (11:30–33)

These verses appear to be a somewhat random inclusion in the flow of chapters 11 and 12. We must ask, then: Why does Paul refer to this particular event?

The event to which Paul refers happened many years before. Paul, as a follower of Jesus, was a wanted man, a high-profile Christian leader. There were people out to kill him. On one occasion when his life was in immediate danger, fellow believers helped him escape the city of Damascus—out through a window just in the nick of time. But why does Paul return now, in this context, to this incident that occurred so many years before?

It reads like an exciting series of events (at least to my mind): there's a bit of drama and espionage, with a Tom Cruise character hurling out the window. We might be imagining a thrilling scene from a James Bond movie (especially if we hum the James Bond theme music), only here it's Paul escaping the clutches of the evil king Aretas. We want to cheer him on and say, "Go, Paul! Good on you! You did it! You got away!"

Is that the point?

Actually, it's the exact opposite. Paul is referring to a time when he was put in a smelly fish basket and lowered unceremoniously out of a window. There would have been nothing dignified about Paul's exit from Damascus. His weakness was absolutely on show.

Right when we expect him to boast of great things in this section, given that he is under fire and the Corinthians are losing confidence in him, when he needs his PR machine to swing into gear and do some damage control, he "boasts" of a time when he was utterly humiliated.

Paul says, "I will boast of the things that show my weakness." In other words, I will boast of a time of great shame and humiliation, of what could well have been perceived as pathetic cowardice. It wasn't, but it could well have been perceived that way.

And so he boasts—of his weakness. This, then, is the immediate context for what we read in the opening of chapter 12: "I must go on boasting. Although there is nothing to be gained, I will go on to visions and revelations from the Lord" (v. 1).

We then read of a specific vision in the next few verses. Finally (we may think), *finally* Paul is going to talk about something impressive, something that will make the Corinthians and the super-apostles sit up and listen.

"I know a man in Christ" (v. 2). Who is this man in Christ? It sounds very vague. Well, we need to read further in this chapter to work out that Paul is actually referring to himself but using the third person in order to do so.

Why would he do that? Why not just come straight out and say that *he*, the apostle Paul, had received this vision, especially because he truly had received it—and now he could at least hold his own in that department with the super-apostles?

In these verses Paul is about to describe something that was given to him, an experience from God, of God, which was amazing. But by describing it in the third person, he is creating a distance between himself and that experience.

It's a bit like what we do when we refer to "a friend," perhaps, if we are talking about something we might be a bit embarrassed or sensitive about. Using the unidentified third person rather than first person keeps the personal connection vague but still allows us to get advice or express anxiety or get something off our chest, so to speak.

For example, I might say something like, "I have 'a friend' who has been known to eat a whole block of chocolate in one sitting." I certainly don't want you to know it's me. By using the third-person term "friend," I have created a distance between myself and this experience, in this case because the experience is one not to be proud of (unless you think eating a whole block of chocolate is an impressive feat).

Paul is doing the opposite here: he is creating a distance between himself and something amazing and awe-inspiring, something that would have been very impressive to the Corinthian Christians. How easy it would have been just to have mentioned, in passing, a few more details about what he has alluded to—especially in the context of being attacked for not being impressive enough.

Here was Paul's opportunity to score some points, and yet

he writes, "I know a man in Christ." Fourteen years before, this man was caught up to the "third heaven" (v. 2), or "paradise" (v. 4). The third heaven and paradise were both ways of describing the very place where the Lord God Almighty dwells. It must have been a truly amazing and awe-inspiring experience.

Whether in the body (that is, transported bodily) or out of the body (that is, transported spiritually), Paul doesn't know. But it doesn't matter. The point is, it happened; it was real.

He was taken up to paradise, where, as he says in verse 4, he heard "inexpressible things," that is, wonderful and exalted things that were impossible to put into words. There were no categories to describe what he heard.

Even if he could have explained what he heard, he was not permitted to tell. In *this* context, God cannot be talked about (remember: context is important!). Of course, there are other records of Paul receiving visions and revelations that he was permitted to tell (see, e.g., Acts 27:21–26). Such visions were given to him to encourage him in very difficult circumstances. It may well be that he had been given these surpassingly great revelations fourteen years before for the same purpose, to encourage him in what he boasts about in 2 Corinthians 11:24–28: shipwreck, flogging, stoning, and so on—all situations in which he was weak and oppressed. But the apostle will not boast about the experience of "a man" caught up to the third heaven, with all its impressiveness and strength, even though it is true and it happened to him.

No, he won't boast of that; he will speak of it, but only in the third person and with no elaboration whatsoever. But he will boast of the man the Corinthian Christians actually knew in their context: Paul himself, in all his weakness. This is the apostle Paul, who never tried to hide his weaknesses from them. He acknowledges that he *could* boast and speak the truth but that he refrains, "so no one will think more of me than is warranted by what I do or say" (12:6).

This is looking through the gospel lens at weakness, difficulty, and opposition—it means *not* boasting about things that make us look great, because then we have our eyes on ourselves rather than on the Lord Jesus Christ who for our sakes made himself nothing. We have our eyes on ourselves rather than on the cross, where Jesus was humbled to the point of death, taking on our sin, in our place.

Sadly, this gospel Paul preached so passionately is too seldom at the center of our thoughts, and so we do not often enough share Paul's perspective on weakness. I, for example, *do* want you to think more of me than is warranted. I *do* want you to think highly of me. I do *want* to tell you about all the things that make me look good—and, at the same time, play down or hide the things that make me look weak.

That's why we have our qualifications framed on our walls. That's why we lend a book that happens to have a personal message from the author—it shows how "connected" we are. That's why we may drop into the conversation that we're going out for dinner with our husband because of his promotion, or what schools our children attend (especially if they're selective ones). We might mention the church we attend because it is a big, well-known one, or the size of the ministry teams we're part of. We might drop into conversation the name of our pastor because we know how well-known he is ("Did you know he even speaks at The Gospel Coalition? Imagine that!").

None of these things is bad in itself; in fact they may all very well be good gifts from God. But we can so easily turn them into tools used to impress others and to make us look good, to give us the glory. It's so easy for us to do that.

With the gospel of Jesus Christ as our GPS, giving the right perspective, we will boast differently. The gospel shapes our boasting; it will end our boasting about things that make us look great.

Recently I read a great little biography of George White-field, famous evangelistic preacher of the 1800s. Concerning the dangers of popularity, Whitefield said this:

> The tide of popularity began to run very high. In a short time I could no longer walk on foot, but was constrained to go in a coach from place to place, to avoid the hosannas of the multitude. They grew quite extravagant in their applauses, and had it not been for my compassionate High Priest, popularity would have destroyed me. I used to plead with him to take me by the hand and lead me unhurt through this fiery furnace. He heard my request and gave me to see the vanity of all commendations but his own.[6]

That's looking at life through the gospel lens, seeing the vanity of all commendations but God's, and not boasting about things that make us look great. How unlike the world this is! The world would tell us to commend ourselves. The gospel tells us that our commendation from God comes not from ourselves but only by the grace of our Lord Jesus Christ.

So *here is our God*, who won't allow himself to be talked about

---

[6] Arnold A. Dallimore, *George Whitefield: God's Anointed Servant in the Great Revival of the Eighteenth Century* (Wheaton, IL: Crossway, 1990), 29.

if it means boasting for our glory and greatness. When we look through the lens of the gospel, our boasting is transformed; we no longer boast about things that make us look great.

So how does the gospel lens change our view of weakness and strength? The first answer has shown how this lens transforms our boasting. The second answer focuses specifically on a transformed view of weakness itself.

2) THE GOSPEL LENS SHOWS OUR WEAKNESS IN A NEW LIGHT (2 COR. 12:7–10)

If we had any doubt that Paul was the "man in Christ" described in 2 Corinthians 12:1–6, it becomes clear now that he is indeed that man—especially when he tells of receiving a strange gift given "to keep me from becoming conceited," "because of these surpassingly great revelations" (v. 7).

These visions and revelations given to Paul fourteen years earlier were clearly still vivid in his mind, surpassingly great and inexpressible. They would have been an amazing encouragement to this hardworking and much-suffering apostle. But there is a danger with such great blessings. The danger is that our human condition can so easily turn them into opportunities for our own glory. To guard against that danger, Paul was given "a thorn."

Now we see why Paul is writing about these revelations "that no one is permitted to tell" (v. 4). He mentions these revelations not as an opportunity to boast surreptitiously; rather, they are simply the context for what Paul really wanted to focus on: his weakness because of the thorn.

When Paul writes in verse 7, "I was given a thorn," we of course want to ask who gave it to him. The answer: God. Paul here writes in what has been called "the divine passive," using the passive form of the verb, avoiding direct reference to God (out of reverence), but at the same time indicating that it was indeed God who performed the action.[7] God gave this thorn to Paul, and he tells us it was given in order to keep him from becoming conceited.

This thorn, also described as a messenger of Satan, was given to him to torment him (v. 7). And it was given at the same time as these surpassingly great revelations fourteen years before. Now, how can this thorn come from God *and* be a messenger of Satan?

There are two principles we need to keep hold of as we think this through.

First, we must never forget that God is sovereign, and nothing happens outside his sovereign will. Nothing. If he ceases to be sovereign at one point, he ceases to be sovereign.

Second, some things happen in this life that are painful and in which it is hard to see any good at all. People get sick, people die, there is chronic disease, accidents happen, there is mental illness, relationships break down, and we feel the strain of going against the flow of life because we are Christians. Life can be hard.

People sometimes talk about terrible things in their life and then wrap it up with a summary statement: "Oh well, it's all good." But it's not always all good.

God is always good, but life is not always easy. There will come a time when there will be no more pain or death or mourning or tears; Revelation 21 reminds us of that. But until then, the hard stuff of this world is a reality.

---

[7] Barnett, *Message of 2 Corinthians*, 178.

Life can be hard. Just as it was for Paul.

Despite many attempts by many biblical scholars over the years to pin down what the thorn was, no one really knows. Perhaps it was physical sickness, perhaps a physical or emotional impediment of some kind, or perhaps even a person or people who made his life hard. We simply don't know. We *do* know that whatever it was, it wasn't good; it was painful.

So great was the torment that Paul pleaded with the Lord for its removal: "Three times I *pleaded* with the Lord to take it away from me" (2 Cor. 12:8). This is the same Paul who endured so much hardship without complaining. In chapter 11, he recounts his sufferings like he's describing what he had for breakfast!

And yet here we read that he pleads three times with the Lord Jesus: "Please, Lord, take it away from me." Jesus's reply to this desperate cry: No. "But he said to me, 'My grace is sufficient for you, for my power is made perfect in weakness'" (v. 9). This was not the answer Paul was looking for. He was looking for relief through the removal of the torment of this thorn.

The subject of suffering is a difficult one. You may be asking even as you read this: Doesn't God want his people to be relieved from torment? Doesn't he want us to be victorious in this life, to be triumphant and powerful and strong and successful? Wouldn't that be a helpful witness to the watching world? Doesn't God promise that he will heal so that with great power we can "fly the flag" of the gospel?

In a word: no. Oh, yes, he knows what we need. He will always do what is right, and he knows what we are like. But he may not take away our suffering. For Paul, the thorn kept him from thinking that he was some kind of spiritual super-man. It reminded him of his weakness, of his humanness. The Lord Jesus Christ said to Paul, and in fact, continued to say,[8] "my grace is sufficient for you, for my power is made perfect in weakness."

Fourteen years after he was first given this thorn, the same words ring true: my grace is sufficient for you. In other words, in the context of weakness, of trials, of difficulties, there would always be sufficient grace, continuing grace, year after year, to bear up under the torment and the difficulties. Paul was not left high and dry.

The same is true for all who know the Lord Jesus. We are not left high and dry either. In fact, the more we are aware of our weakness, the more evident and obvious is Christ's enabling strength. His strength means that we *can* bear up under the hard stuff.

This was Paul's experience: "Therefore I will boast all the more gladly about my weaknesses, so that Christ's power may rest on me. That is why, for Christ's sake, I delight in weak-nesses, in insults, in hardships, in persecutions, in difficulties. For when I am weak, then I am strong" (vv. 9–10). It's like he is saying, "Bring it on!" Paul is no masochist, nor is he a stoic. It is not a matter of having the British "stiff upper lip," or embracing the spirit of the ANZACs by digging your heels in, or simply taking an aspirin and soldiering on![9]

No, it is *Christ's strength* in the context of our weakness. This is what Paul wanted the Corinthian Christians to under-stand. As we look through the lens of the gospel, this is what

---

[8] The NIV translation has "said," but a more literal translation would be "says."
[9] ANZAC is the acronym for Australian and New Zealand Army Corps, comprising troops who fought in World War I in the Battle of Gallipoli.

we see: power in weakness. Paul spells it out beautifully in 2 Corinthians 13:4: "For to be sure, [Jesus] was crucified in weakness, yet he lives by God's power. Likewise, we are weak in him, yet by God's power we will live."

Power in weakness: that is Paul's experience because that is how God works. As we track the history of God's people, there is a consistent witness of God's power in the context of weak and often disappointing people. To choose just one of many possible examples, consider the disciples of Jesus: not exactly the "who's who" of the religious establishment, so often getting it wrong, so often confused about who Jesus was and why he came into this world. When we look back at the cloud of witnesses through the centuries, we find a consistent witness of Christ's power made perfect in weakness.

What we're talking about is what Paul talks about in 1 Corinthians 1:27–29: "But God chose the foolish things of the world to shame the wise; God chose the weak things of the world to shame the strong. God chose the lowly things of this world and the despised things—and the things that are not—to nullify the things that are, so that no one may boast before him."

Christ's power shines in human weakness.

This was the testimony of John Bunyan, author of *Pilgrim's Progress*, who also wrote of his experience of power made perfect in weakness. Bunyan was an English minister and preacher in the 1600s. He was imprisoned because of the gospel, leaving his family bereft of husband and father, with his heart breaking for them all. From prison Bunyan wrote this:

> I never had in all my life so great an inlet into the Word of God as now. The Scriptures that I saw nothing in before,

are made in this place to shine upon me. Jesus Christ also was never more real and apparent than now. Here I have seen him and felt him indeed . . . being very tender of me, God would with one Scripture after another strengthen me against all. . . . I have often said, were it lawful I could pray for greater trouble, for greater comfort's sake.[10]

These are remarkable words: "Were it lawful I could pray for greater trouble, for greater comfort's sake." In other words, bring it on!

Such an attitude doesn't make sense from a human perspective, but that's because our perspective is so limited. We see so little. We don't have the whole picture. God is working out his purposes for his glory and our good and showing himself to us in ways we would never expect or choose. Indeed, *this is our God*!

What grace that we can know this God even, perhaps especially, in times when we feel most weak, no matter the nature of our "thorns," whether disappointment with the way life is turning out, sickness, loneliness, insecurity, or fear for the future. These are the times when the Lord softens our hearts, working on them like a farmer turning soil prepared for seed. The times when we feel weak are opportunities to understand in greater measure the love, the grace, and the strength of the Lord Jesus Christ.

These are the times when, in weakness, we are driven to depend on God alone, and in that dependence we find he satisfies the deepest longings of our hearts. We learn to trust God like never before. We see him more clearly than ever before.

---

[10] John Bunyan, *Grace Abounding to the Chief of Sinners* (Hertfordshire, UK: Evangelical Press, 1978), 123.

In our weakness, we are stripped of our delusions of competence, of depending on our own abilities. Just as it happened for John Bunyan in his time of need, the truths of God—of his love and grace—invade our hearts. Knowing this makes me more willing to lower my facade of "having it all together." It makes me willing to be honest about what seems weak to me and what I don't want anyone to know, in case they think less of me.

We all work so hard to put forward a picture of confidence, of happiness, of strength, of abilities, of success. We work hard to be "shiny happy people" (to quote the title of the REM song of 1991). But at the same time, we are all acutely aware of our own weaknesses. We just work hard to make sure no one else can see them.

It's often not easy to talk about our weaknesses. I don't really want you to know that I have never been to university—not when education is so highly thought of in our world today. I don't really want you to know that I am a slow reader and that it takes me a while to get through books. I want you to think I am clever and intelligent. I don't really want you to know that the very thought of writing a chapter for a book terrifies me. I want you to think that this is all part of my daily work.

But when I am thinking in line with the gospel, I know that the Lord is not limited by what *I* can bring to the table in service to him. "Nothing in my hand I bring, simply to the cross I cling."[11] Looking through the lens of the gospel, we see that we bring nothing, and Christ brings everything on our behalf.

Oh, God gives us gifts to use and great opportunities to

---

[11] A. M. Toplady, "Rock of Ages," 1763.

use them! But if we think that who we are and what we do is impressive in itself, then we are beginning to travel down the road those super-apostles were on, delighting in their strengths and seeking their own glory.

No, we serve a God who will not share his glory with anyone but who delights to use us in our weakness. Here is our God, who reveals himself to his servants in amazing ways and for some, in inexpressible ways.

Here is our God, who teaches us in our weakness, who gives us grace to live in this world, providing all that we need—even in suffering making us more than conquerors through him who loved us (Rom. 8:37).

Here is our God, who wants us to serve him and live for him where he has placed us now, not so that we will get the glory, and not so that people will be impressed by us, but all for the glory of Christ who died for us and was raised to life.

Here is our God, who came into this world and lived the gospel paradox: crucified in weakness but resurrected in God's power.

We have been given a paradoxical life to live—life that boasts in weakness because weakness knows the power of God. That's the gospel perspective.

FINAL REFLECTIONS ON THIS GOSPEL LENS

We look at ourselves and the world and think we see clearly: strength, power, success, popularity, wealth—that's the way to go! But then we read this passage in 2 Corinthians 12, we put on the gospel lens, and everything comes into focus. Through Christ, we see that weakness is not to be despised but embraced.

With gospel eyes we will delight in weakness, not because it's a comfortable place to be but because it is the showcase of God's power. Weakness is the place from which we can say, "Here is our God!" It is the place where we know his amazing grace and all-sufficiency, a place where, stripped of all our supposed strengths and supports, we experience—more than that, we *rest in*—the grace of the Lord Jesus Christ.

This is our confidence indeed: "He was crucified in weakness, yet he lives by God's power. Likewise, we are weak in him, yet by God's power we will live" (2 Cor. 13:4).

REFLECTION AND DISCUSSION QUESTIONS

1) What various aspects of God are revealed to Paul and through Paul to us, in 2 Corinthians 12?

2) Think back over the previous passages in which we have seen God show himself in spectacular ways (Exodus 19; 1 Kings 8; Isaiah 6; Psalm 40; and Matt. 17:1–15). How does Paul show in 2 Corinthians 12 that he knows and is motivated by the God revealed in each of those passages?

3) Paul shows us *how* to proclaim, "Here is your God!" What phrases from 2 Corinthians 12 stand out in showing us Paul's method of proclamation? Which phrases challenge you most personally?

4) How is the person and work of Jesus Christ central to the message of 2 Corinthians 12? (See also 2 Cor. 13:3–4.)

5) Jenny Salt is honest in challenging us, practically, to follow Paul's example of boasting only in the Lord. In what ways does the church today—and do we today—need to hear this challenge?

7

Through the Open Door

THE TRANSCENDENT AND REDEEMING GOD

Revelation 4–5

KATHLEEN NIELSON

We have seen God reveal himself on a fiery mountain, in a shining temple, in the vision of a heavenly throne room, in a miry swamp, on another mountain where Jesus shines, in a third heaven Paul couldn't talk about, and, now, in the lit-up courts of heaven—which John was not only permitted but instructed to talk about.

The book of Revelation lets us see God in a way that's meant to light up our whole lives to the end. It's not a new seeing; Revelation is the culmination of all the other visions of God throughout Scripture. But it's a *big* vision—a vision that encompasses the panorama of human history. We're ambitious to look into two chapters, Revelation 4 and 5. Yet we wouldn't want to leave one without the other; they go together. When we were planning the conference plenary topics, Don Carson commented on these two chapters, saying they belong together, for chapter 4 sets the stage, and chapter 5 unpacks the drama. I wrote that down, just in case I might want to remember it. I'm glad I did. It helps! And it's true: Revelation 4 sets the stage, with the God of creation on his throne. And Revelation 5 develops the drama, as Christ the Lamb of God comes to that throne. There are two chapters, but there is one theme: that *the creator-redeemer God reigns*. And there is only one response: to *worship* him.

REVELATION 4: WHERE?

Let's get at all this by taking in the words as carefully as we can. We'll simply ask five questions about each chapter, beginning with the question, Where? Where are we, as we approach the book of Revelation? We have to give a few different answers to this question, and the first, obvious answer is that *we're at the end of the Bible*! We call Revelation the consummation of the Bible's story line: it's the coming together of all the threads that wind around one another from Genesis on, in this big story of God's redeeming a people for himself through his Son. Maybe one reason Revelation is such a hard book for us is that we don't know well enough the whole rest of the Bible. We are so much more ready to enter this heavenly scene if we've glimpsed it already with Isaiah, in Isaiah 6. And if we had time to go back and visit this same scene with Ezekiel and Daniel, we'd be even more ready. We'll trace some of those threads. So where are we? We're at the end of the whole Bible.

But where are we *in this book*? Here's a second answer: *we're in the midst of persecution.* The historical context of Revelation is one of horrific persecution of Christians under first-century Roman emperors such as Nero and Domitian. The apostle John as he writes is imprisoned on the island of Patmos, and he's there (according to Rev. 1:9) "on account of the word of God and the testimony of Jesus." In chapters 2–3, John writes letters to churches that are under great persecution, and he tells of more to come. Knowing this context of persecution helps us grasp the purpose of the book, which is not just to reveal end times, not just to satisfy our curiosity about what's coming. The purpose of Revelation is to encourage God's people to persevere in faith to the end, even through suffering and persecution. So where are we, in this book? We're at the end of the Bible, and we're in the midst of persecution. We're reading words of encouragement to the first-century persecuted church.

But where are we *personally* in this book? How can we connect now, today? Where are *we* in this book? Here's a third answer: *we're linked in to a blessed chain of recipients.* The book opens like this:

> The revelation of Jesus Christ, which God gave him to show to his servants the things that must soon take place. He made it known by sending his angel to his servant John, who bore witness to the word of God and to the testimony of Jesus Christ, even to all that he saw. (1:1–2)

Now, we could say a lot of things about those verses, but one thing we're sure to notice is that there's a revelation being passed on. The revelation is clearly all about Jesus: this is "the revelation of Jesus Christ." But in that first sentence Jesus becomes not just the subject of the revelation; there in verse 1 Jesus is also the receiver and the revealer of the revelation: "The revelation of Jesus Christ, which God gave to him [Jesus] to show to his servants." In the first two verses the whole chain of revelation includes these links: first, God (God is the initiator), to Jesus Christ, through an angel, to John, to God's servants. So when John, down in verse 4, starts giving this revelation ("John, to the seven churches that are in Asia"), we know this is not just a message from him. The chain of revelation stretches far back, all the way back to God.

It stretches forward as well. This is not just a message to seven little churches. The chain stretches far in both directions; in fact, it stretches forward all the way to us. How do we know that?

We'll talk in a minute about symbolism, but at this point let's just note that the number seven in Revelation symbolizes perfection or completeness. As you read through Revelation, you notice right away that it's a book full of sevens—seven trumpets, seven seals, seven bowls of wrath—and that number seven always symbolizes perfect completeness. So these seven churches to whom John writes are evidently meant to symbolize, or represent, the complete church—first in John's time but by implication *all* of it in *all* times. We today are part of the present link in this chain, part of the whole church down through the ages. That means this book is for us personally, Christ's body, his people, still today facing suffering and persecution all over the world. That's where we are in this book—not on the outside listening dispassionately but on the inside, *linked in*.

You can go online these days and get "LinkedIn" to a network of professionals; well, this is the original and the best kind of "linked in," to the source of it all. As believers we are linked-in recipients in this chain of revelation initiated by God himself and passed down through Christ himself, through an angel, through John, to the church—and so to us.

The wonderful promise is that this revelation from God keeps sending a blessing down through all the links, to all the ones who receive it. The links are live! Revelation 1:3 makes a promise: "Blessed is the one who reads aloud the words of this prophecy, and blessed are those who hear, and who keep what is written in it, for the time is near." According to that verse, we are blessed to hear and privileged to receive this part of God's Word. So where are we? We're at the end of the Bible, in the context of the persecuted church, and linked in to a blessed chain of recipients.

But where are we specifically in chapter 4? Here's a fourth and final answer to "Where?" *We're in heaven.* In Revelation 4:1, John sees a door standing open *in heaven* and hears calling him the same trumpet-like voice he heard back in verse 10 of chapter 1, which was the voice of Jesus. At once, John says, he was "in the Spirit"; that is, God's Spirit leads him into this vision. We don't know the details of *how* (just like Paul didn't and couldn't know, in 2 Cor. 12:2–4), but we do know that John, in the Spirit, clearly enters this door and immediately describes a throne "in heaven." We're in *heaven*, in this scene. It's a place we glimpse through the prophets, a place Jesus talked about all the time, a place Paul wasn't allowed to talk about. But how amazing: here we get to enter heaven's throne room through a vision that actually took John there and gave him the words to describe it to us.

Even just this much blesses us, the fact that this vision gives us access to realities that are invisible and yet so close. It's these invisible things that require faith, right? Faith, "the conviction of things not seen" (Heb. 11:1). Isn't it wonderful that the picture here is of a door standing open? It's not a picture of flying far away to a distant place. No, it's right there, just across the threshold. The Bible gives all sorts of hints of the invisible reality that is right there, to be seen in a flash whenever God chooses to pull up the veil. God did it for Elisha and his servant, when Elisha prayed that the Lord would open his servant's eyes, and suddenly his servant saw those heavenly horses and chariots of fire in the mountains all around (2 Kings 6:17). God did it for Stephen right before he was stoned, as Stephen cried out, "Behold, I see the heavens opened, and the Son of Man standing at the right hand of God!" (Acts 7:55–56).

Most of the time we don't get to see these invisible realities. But we do begin to glimpse them through revelation, God's *unveiling in words* so that we can begin to see what is invisible. The whole Bible is God's revelation to us, in that sense, but this final book is a special kind, a special genre of revelation named after the Greek word for revelation, *apokalypsis*. The book of Revelation is *apocalyptic* prophecy, which means it unveils heavenly realities through these words sent from God. Often it unveils *future* heavenly realities. The book's opening line promises to show "the things that must soon take place." Here in chapter 4 John hears a call to come up and see "what must take place after this" (v. 1). There's a huge sense of anticipation from the start: these words from God will unveil not only heavenly realities that exist right now but also future realities. This apocalyptic prophecy will unveil a heavenly plan for human history into the future and into eternity.

Where are we, then, as we approach Revelation 4? We're at the end of the Bible; we're in the context of the persecuted church; we're linked in live to a blessed chain of recipients; and we're taken with John into heaven, where invisible realities are unveiled for us through these inspired words.

REVELATION 4: WHAT?

You might have expected the second question would be, Who? But think for a moment: how would we answer the question of who appears in this vision? The obvious answer is "God." But how do we see God? What does he look like in this vision? What might we say first about him, just from chapter 4? We'd probably say he's sitting on a throne. In fact, in verse 2 the throne is mentioned even before the one seated on it. And here we come to a main distinctive of apocalyptic literature: the *what* question will interpret the *who* question, and in fact all the other questions. That's because apocalyptic literature works through *pictures*—so *what we see* is the thing. And what we see are pictures, symbolic pictures, of everything and everybody. That's why we'll first ask, What? and then we'll ask, Who?

We're not always comfortable coming at truth through pictures—especially we Western outline-loving, logical thinkers. I like outlines. A logical outline can make us feel like we're in control of a bunch of facts, like we've distilled them into a manageable shape, like we feel when we've got all the unruly kids tucked in to bed. But here's the point: there's no logical outline that can get us even close to the reality of who God is.

There's no way we could ever get it all tucked in. Pictures, however—symbolic word pictures—don't distill but rather *expand* our comprehension as we keep imagining and seeing more and more vividly.

The book of Revelation gives us anything but a logical outline; instead, it gives us a magnificent array of pictures to ponder. One picture doesn't even need to work logically with another. Did you ever have an English teacher somewhere in the distant past who told you not to mix your metaphors? In heaven you can mix metaphors and nobody cares. A figure can be both a lion and a lamb. The point is not to make the pictures relate logically. The point is certainly not to draw the pictures literally. The point is to see the array of pictures given to us in these words, to ponder them, to take them in deeply. The point, really, is that in our humanness we simply cannot imagine the *what* of these heavenly realities, and so this apocalyptic symbolism, which puts pictures of things we recognize together in ways we *don't* recognize, at least gives us clues.

How merciful of God to let us see through pictures, as best we can, until we can bear to see him face-to-face, when we shall be like him and see him as he is. These pictures make us taste and long for that seeing. They say the picture books little children spend hours poring over affect their minds and their development in dramatic ways. Well, we are all children in relation to heaven, and we need to pore over these pictures with everything in us.

The huge *what* of these pictures is the throne; it's the first thing John tells us about (v. 2), and it's mentioned seventeen times in these two chapters. So what does the throne look like? Well, we're not told. We could never draw it. But what does the throne *symbolize*? It symbolizes the sovereign rule of God. If we tried to sketch this whole scene, it might look like one of those graph templates we use to plan furniture placement in a room: we'd mark the throne in the very center, and we'd have all these layers of other things placed around it. It's hard to tell just exactly where everything would go, but one thing is certain: everything would be placed in relation to the throne at the center. That's really the point. That's the big thing this picture of heaven teaches us. Everything exists in relation to the throne, the constant reference point, at the very center, always in view. This is the picture we want to carry away from these chapters, because this picture affects the way we plan the templates for our lives.

But let's fill in the picture. The *what* is first and foremost the throne, but the text gives us six layers of pictures that help us process the meaning of the throne and the one seated on it. Let's uncover these layers in the text. First, in verse 3 we meet a brilliant layer of reflective beauty, with these precious stones—jasper and carnelian at the center picturing the one sitting on the throne, and an emerald picturing the rainbow that circles the throne. All the way through the Scriptures there is a path, a tantalizing path of gems. We don't have time to trace it, but we could start, for example, way back in Exodus with the high priest's breastplate inset with twelve precious stones (28:15–21). The path reaches a magnificent end in Revelation 21, as we shall see.

What are all these precious stones doing, pictured as they are in the presence of God? They're *reflecting*. We shouldn't picture stones cut like they are today; not until a couple centuries ago were precious stones cut and clarified as we know them. These would be natural stones deep and rich with color, having no light of their own but shimmering with the light of the one they're all reflecting like a rainbow of color. Of course, the rainbow itself appears here in verse 3, reflecting as well, as rainbows reflect a whole spectrum of colors from the sun. All this luminous color is reflecting and shining forth God's majesty. These glorious precious stones give just a hint of God's glorious being. That rainbow "around the throne" suggests the whole spectrum of his being, including his covenant-making mercy given back in the time of Noah and reaching to the very end.

We're drawn by this beauty, aren't we? We sort of lean in, pulled in by such precious stones and shimmering colors. We might recall in 2011 the whole world leaning in with dazzled concentration to see Kate Middleton's gorgeous eighteen-carat, deep-blue, sapphire-and-diamond, oval engagement ring, the same one the world had leaned in to see on the hand of Princess Diana. What a magnetic draw in one sparkling ring, admired and copied all over the globe. Of course that's just a poor suggestion of the gems we encounter here in Revelation, which draw us in to the center of this scene with its shimmering throne.

Even as these pictures pull us in, however, the very language of the description tells us we can't get at this directly. It says the one seated on the throne *had the appearance of* jasper and carnelian, and the rainbow *had the appearance of an emerald*. The words, even while *showing* us, kind of *separate* us from the real thing. We have to use the pictures, and remember that we're using pictures—until it's time to see him face-to-face. Ezekiel does the same thing: after a quite similar description of the heavenly throne and gems and rainbow, Ezekiel 1 ends with an amazing sentence that points to God's glory but keeps us grammatically at least four steps away from it: "Such was the appearance of the likeness of the glory of the LORD" (v. 28).

The second layer of the *what* sort of interrupts our leaning in. The second layer "around the throne" (Rev. 4:4) is the ring of twenty-four thrones with twenty-four white-clothed, golden-crowned elders seated on them. We could spend a lot of time trying to decide who these elders are, but we won't. Are they perhaps a circle of saints representing all of God's people, twelve tribes in the Old Testament and twelve apostles in the New Testament, totaling twenty-four? That's a significant correspondence. Do they perhaps reflect the twenty-four orders of Old Testament priests (1 Chron. 24:7–19)? Another and a very good option mentioned by many is that these elders are a high order of angelic beings surrounding God's throne, sort of like royal heavenly courtiers, whom God's people perhaps reflect in all their earthly ordering.[1]

It's challenging to ask whether these heavenly pictures reflect earthly reality or whether the earthly reflects the heavenly. We tend to want to start with what we know—sort of like assuming the earth is the center of the galaxy, with all the planets revolving around us. Revelation is indeed like a

---

[1] I have found the following five theologians particularly helpful, not only in their discussion of the twenty-four elders but in their overall commentary on the book of Revelation: G. K. Beale, *The Book of Revelation: A Commentary on the Greek Text* (Grand Rapids, MI: Eerdmans, 1999); D. A. Carson, in a series of lectures on Revelation, http://thegospelcoalition.org/resources/scripture-index/a/revelation; James M. Hamilton Jr., *Revelation: The Spirit Speaks to the Churches*, Preaching the Word, ed. R. Kent Hughes (Wheaton, IL: Crossway, 2012); Dennis E. Johnson, *Triumph of the Lamb: A Commentary on Revelation* (Phillipsburg, NJ: P&R, 2001); Vern S. Poythress, *The Returning King: A Guide to the Book of Revelation* (Phillipsburg, NJ: P&R, 2000).

spiritual Copernican revolution, with heaven as the center. Everything else exists in relation to this. This is the heavenly throne room, the original, the real one! It might make us recall Solomon's temple in 1 Kings 8 and those carved cherubim with their wings spreading over the ark of the covenant. Those carved figures reflected the sorts of heavenly creatures we're seeing here in action, flying around the throne. That earthly temple, Hebrews tells us, contained copies of heavenly things (9:23). The Scriptures pull us to understand earth in terms of heaven, not heaven in terms of earth. The Scriptures pull us toward the throne of heaven as our ultimate reference point.

It makes sense in many ways that these twenty-four elders should be heavenly beings; in subsequent chapters they are clearly distinguished from the saints, as we'll see even in Revelation 5 (v. 8), where the elders join a song of redemption referring not to themselves but to others as the ransomed people of God.

This heavenly picture in chapter 4 is all *other*, all different from us. The sense of awe for the other is heightened by the next layers of what we see; they pile on quickly, one phrase after another, to create an overwhelming impression of awesomeness. The third layer (v. 5) consists of lightning flashes and peals of thunder—this time not "around the throne" but actually "from the throne." From the throne at the center come these flashings and thunderings that make the whole scene fearful and awesome like ones we have seen before. We have visited Mount Sinai with Moses, back in Exodus 19, with the thunder and lightning and even the trumpet blast, so that all the people in the camp trembled. Here we are *in* the throne room, in the presence of the very source of the storm.

Do lightning and thunder make you tremble? I live on a mountain. It's only a little mountain, but even on our little Lookout Mountain, Georgia, when thunderstorms come we just feel so exposed, especially at the mountain's very top, where our college's main building sits, with a tower that seems to reach right up into the sky. When we are on the very top of our mountain, the thunderstorms don't seem to go *by* us over our head; they seem to come right *to* us across the sky. The streaks of lightning split open the clouds next to us, and the thunder is right there, like the finale of the fireworks that you feel vibrating deep in your gut.

Along with the thunder and lightning comes the next and fourth layer, these seven torches of fire burning "before the throne" (Rev. 4:5). We must keep noticing that everything is described in relation to the throne. We're told these seven torches are the seven spirits of God, which throughout the book seem to be John's consistent picture for the Holy Spirit. We know the number seven symbolizes perfection. It makes sense here to picture the Holy Spirit as perfect and complete even while manifested in a variety of places and ways. There's light and fire flashing through this whole scene. As you come to these torches right on the heels of the thunder and lightning in the text, it almost seems as if the lightning streaks from the throne right into the torches, these fiery torches that both draw us and yet separate us from the throne.

That sense of separation grows with the next phrase in verse 6: another layer, a fifth one, again "before the throne." It's not exactly a sea of glass; it's "as it were a sea of glass, like crystal." Apocalyptic writing might be one of the few contexts conducive to that irritating plague of the word *like* that has invaded the English language. So what is this? "Well, it's like, a sea. It's like, crystal." There's no way to say directly what this is! Ezekiel saw it, too, this same shining expanse. It clearly reflects God's shining glory. Some see it simply as a picture of peace, but here's a great example of how biblical context is important. Throughout the Bible, the sea is not our friend; it's consistently associated with chaos and evil. Have you noticed how many psalms celebrate God's power to put and keep the seas within their bounds? Think of the picture of God's deliverance through the parting of the Red Sea. Later in Revelation, from where does the beast come? From out of the sea. Revelation 21 will picture a new heaven and a new earth without any sea. For now, though, the sea is still there, but it's completely subject to God's throne. I like that: all chaos, all threat just stretched out before and completely in subjection to the throne of God.

The sixth and final layer of the *what* comes with these four living creatures who are all "around the throne, on each side of the throne" (4:6). Four figures make us think of north, south, east, and west. They are everywhere; they're in motion, dozens of wings whirling around the throne in all directions, just as the eyes all over them show the all-seeing, omniscient God they surround and reflect and continually praise. If you have been reading Isaiah 6, you know creatures similar to these. The prophet Ezekiel describes amazingly similar creature, although each of his four creatures has four faces and shining whirling wheels. In spite of some differences, though, these living creatures are always near the throne, close to God, and so reflect most dramatically the being of the Lord God. God's glory here is being reflected through these pictures of all he created: a lion reflects his royal splendor; an ox shows his power; a man reflects the Creator's very image; an eagle in flight reflects his majestic swiftness.

REVELATION 4: WHO?

And now we're ready for the question, Who? What does this *what* (all six layers of it) show us about the *who*? What do all these layers around the throne show us about the one sitting on it? The main answer comes there in verse 8, in the ongoing hymn of praise sung by these living creatures: it's that this is the holy, holy, holy Lord God Almighty. We have been learning about God's holiness through these various passages in which God shows himself to us. We learned much from Isaiah 6, the only other biblical passage that lets us hear this cry of "Holy, holy, holy!" We know that holiness has to do with transcendence, otherness, and perfect righteousness. It's hard to define holiness except to say, as John Piper has said, that holiness is what God is. There is indeed nothing else but God according to which we can define *holy*; we can only repeat it over and over.

But we've been peering into it here in Revelation 4. All these layers around the throne have shown us not only the shining glory of God's holiness; they have shown us as well how far *separated* we are from that holiness, separated by fire, by a vast sea, by circles of royal servants, and by creatures so strange to us that we cannot begin to tame them in our imaginations. God's holiness is shimmering out from the center of this heavenly scene through layers of strange, shining, burning reflections of himself—his holy, holy, holy self.

Notice that God's holiness is directly connected to his eternal nature: "Holy, holy, holy is the Lord God Almighty, *who was and is and is to come!*" The same idea repeats in verse 9, with the phrase "who lives forever and ever," and then again in verse 10: "who lives forever and ever." It's almost like another "Holy, holy, holy." Consider this connection: God is holy; God is *God* because he has *eternal life in himself.* This is what sets him apart. Everything else that lives, lives only with life derived from him. God has *eternal* life; we created beings have only *derived* life, life totally dependent on our creator. To talk about ourselves as even existing apart from our creator does not make sense. It makes sense, then, that the final lines of praise in this chapter focus on God as creator. From the beginning he has been God on his throne; every created thing exists only in relation to the Creator at the center, who made all of it.

REVELATION 4: WHY AND WHEN?

Two more questions are left to ask, for chapter 4. We've asked where and what and who. We need to ask, Why? Why, as in, What's the point? There's only one answer to that question: *worship.* What's going on here at the end of this scene? In verse 10, the twenty-four elders fall down before him who is seated on the throne and *worship* him who lives forever and ever. They cast their crowns before him, acknowledging their utter dependence on him as sovereign creator and ruler. They declare his worthiness, his God-ness, acknowledging in words all that belongs to him because of his very being: glory and honor and power. Their words reflect him here just like the precious stones and the creatures and everything else in this scene, reflecting the almighty creator God who reigns.

The final question is, When? When is this heavenly scene taking place? Chapter 5 will better answer this question, but for now let's answer with, "Now." You recall John has been promised that these visions will show "what must take place after this." That implies the future, but in fact the unfolding of the future doesn't begin until right *after* these heavenly scenes in chapters 4–5. We have first to see the drama around this throne, and only then (only after chapter 5) are we ready to see the plans for human history sent out from this throne. Those plans will take the rest of the book. The rest of the book flows out of the high point of these two chapters—from the *throne*.

Let's never forget that this heavenly scene, with God's throne at the center, is the center of the universe *now*, with this ongoing worship of our creator God. There is a throne in heaven now, awesome and sovereign. Don't doubt it. It's right there right now as if just through a door. Let's think of this throne when we wake up tomorrow morning. Let's never sing the doxology again without thinking about this ongoing heavenly praise we're joining: "Praise him above, ye heavenly host!" Let's never think about our sufferings or our joys—or others' sufferings and joys—without letting live in our imaginations the picture of this sovereign throne and our awesome holy God and this worship of him ringing right now at the center of the universe.

If we stopped here, with chapter 4, we would learn a great deal, but we would miss the drama that actually enables us to *participate* in the worship of heaven. We said (or, rather, we quoted Don Carson as saying) that chapter 4 sets the stage and chapter 5 unpacks the drama. In chapter 4, where is John?

He's an observer and recorder. In chapter 5, John becomes a passionate participant. I studied chapter 4 and was filled with awe but also with a kind of distance and longing. Doesn't chapter 4 pull you and make you long to come in somehow? We need to hear chapter 5 in order to begin to understand both the longing and the utter fulfillment of that longing.

REVELATION 5: WHERE AND WHAT?

Let's ask the same questions again, much more briefly this time. The question *where* won't take long, because we're in the same place. That's important, because what we've just learned about this place and about the one on the throne in the center of it determines the drama of this chapter. We begin and end chapter 5 just as we began and ended chapter 4: looking to the throne.

But there's a new answer to *what*. The huge *what* of this chapter appears right away, there in the right hand of the one seated on the throne: this scroll, this heavenly book rolled up and sealed with seven seals. (Again that number symbolizes completion; the scroll is completely, perfectly sealed shut.) Now, what makes a drama is a crisis, and the crisis here comes in the remarkable moment of tension in verse 2 when that strong angel sends his loud question ringing into the universe: "Who is worthy to open the scroll?" It's as if all of heaven pauses, in silence, for the answer, which comes in verse 3: No one. No one in heaven or on earth or under the earth. No one anywhere. So what is this scroll, what does it mean to be worthy to open it, and why does John begin to weep loudly at the prospect of its not being opened?

The context of Scripture helps, for there are other scrolls, other books, that give us clues. The prophet Ezekiel received a scroll as well, which God told him to eat! Daniel in his vision received a book, which in Daniel 12:4 he's told to close: "Shut up the words and seal the book, until the time of the end." These books symbolize God's decrees for human history. This one here at the end, like Ezekiel's scroll, has writing not just on one side (as would normally have been the case) but on both sides, even on the rough side of those commonly used papyrus strips—the side much more difficult to inscribe. There are no blank spaces in God's plans for us. In fact, every last space is needed for the fullness of God's plans, for every last detail of his perfect decrees for the unfolding of history.

We begin, then, to grasp the horror of this scroll's not being opened, which would mean that human history would not unfold according to God's decrees. Think of it: history cycling randomly at the mercy of human whim or evil, chaotically hurtling toward some unknown end or toward nothing. What if there were no point or meaning in the end? It is good for us to imagine this sense of horror or despair, because this is the very sense that permeates the world in which we live and that explains the despair we find in people all around us. What if there is no larger purpose that gives meaning to any one day, no ultimate justice that will make all things right? Our universe is full of weeping, and all the weeping echoes the weeping of John in this heavenly scene, at the prospect of a universe cut off from God—ultimately a universe without a redeemer to accomplish God's purposes for his creation.

That's really what it means to open the scroll, to break the royal seals: not just to reveal the plans inside, but to have the

authority to bring those plans to pass. The one worthy to reveal and accomplish these plans would have to be as worthy as
the one who decreed them. And that's the point. The drama is
crying out for a worthy hero to resolve this crisis. The whole
universe is crying out for him in this scene.

REVELATION 5: WHO?

Which brings us to the question, Who? The whole drama
turns on the moment of resolution to the crisis, when one
of the elders tells John to weep no more and points to the
huge central figure of this scene. Even as we move to asking
who, we never leave *what* behind in this apocalyptic writing.
He's not called Jesus Christ here; the names used for him are
pictures from Old Testament prophecies that tell us who Jesus
is and what he did for us. These are pictures come to life! In
verse 5, the "Lion of the tribe of Judah" takes us back to Genesis 49:8–10, where dying Jacob blessed his twelve sons and
called Judah a lion, a victorious ruler from whom the scepter
would not depart—Judah, of course, being the tribe from
which Jesus would come, in the line of David.

Through that line the first picture connects with the second one in verse 5, this "Root of David." As we've seen, the
prophet Isaiah pictured the Messiah as a shoot coming from
the stump of Jesse (6:13; 11:1). Isaiah also, however, called
him the *root* of Jesse—that is, the *source* of the promised seed
(11:10). So in Revelation 5, here he is: not just the promised
king descended from David, but *the* eternal king from whom
David came—from whom David and every other earthly king
came. This is the eternal king of heaven. He is the only one
who can approach the throne and take the scroll, as he pro-

ceeds to do in this scene, and who can open the seals, as he'll do in the subsequent chapters, revealing, as the voice said, what *must* take place.

But there's a third name, a third picture that lasts the whole rest of the chapter and the rest of the book. John looks to this figure in verse 6 and sees right there in the center of everything a lamb: "a Lamb standing, as though it had been slain." This is the lion of whom we've just heard, the promised king. But as John looks, he sees a lamb. Now, we don't have to look back and forth and try to make sense of this; John evidently doesn't. It's not like there's a lion and then a lamb, or a lion and a lamb. The lion *is* the Lamb. Perhaps the key question is: How did this conquering lion conquer? The Lamb is the key. The Lamb who was slain.

The key, and the glory, of this conquering figure is that he died. What we see in this scene where the whole course of human destiny is at stake is that everything depends on the Lamb's death. His resurrection from that death is clear: he's a Lamb *standing*. His power is clear, through these seven horns that symbolize perfect, powerful rule. He has conquered! His complete omniscience—and his pervading Spirit—are vividly pictured by these seven eyes, sent out into all the earth just as the Spirit of the risen Christ is sent even now. But the central truth of this figure, the truth that heaven sings about, is that he is a Lamb *slain*. This is the ultimate sacrificial Lamb, who bore our sins in his body on the tree, the one on whom the wrath of God was poured, so that through his death we might live.

This scene reminds us in a climactic way that the gospel is the message of the cross. We might think of Paul's aim to know nothing except Jesus Christ and him crucified (1 Cor. 2:2). We might think of Jesus's words to his disciples about why he came: not to be served but to serve and to give his life as a ransom for many (Mark 10:45). Well, Jesus did what he came to do. And so here we are in heaven hearing songs of praise for the one who did it:

> Worthy are you to take the scroll
>   and to open its seals,
> for you were slain, and by your blood
>   you ransomed people for God. (Rev. 5:9)

Let's just stop and glory in this *who*, this Lamb slain to ransom us, to purchase us for God. This is our redeemer, the Lord Jesus Christ, the great *who* of God's whole revelation. Revelation 4 focused on God our *creator*; chapter 5 completes the story by focusing on God our *redeemer*—through his Son. The song to the Creator in chapter 4 becomes a *new* song to the Redeemer in chapter 5. We need both chapters to get the full theme, that the creator-redeemer God reigns. The beauty is that the Redeemer of chapter 5 does not replace the Creator of chapter 4, just like the Lamb doesn't replace the lion. The Redeemer here takes his place with God to receive the worship of heaven; this is the glorified, ascended, enthroned Son of God at the right hand of the Father. This is the Godhead: Father and Son and Spirit sent out to God's people, through whom we even now join in this heavenly worship. This is one creator-redeemer God. Creation, in fact, is not left behind here; what is redemption but *new* creation—re-creation—a continuing song but a *new* song, to God and to the Lamb.

REVELATION 5: WHEN AND WHY?

We're almost ready for the *why*, but on the way to *why* we're actually dealing with *when*. Chapter 5 shows conclusively that the *when* of this scene is now. This scene pictures heaven now, between Christ's first coming and his coming again. This is the *now* in which we live. According to the Scriptures Christ has died, he has risen, and he has ascended into heaven to sit at God's right hand to reign over the events of human history until he comes again. This "now" is not a permanent state; it's an ongoing story moving quickly toward the end, as the following chapters show. The now of this scene is a now in motion, full of growing praise and worship that's gradually filling the universe. It grows in the text just like we see it growing now, in our time, even in the midst of persecution, as all the nations are coming to know and join in the worship of this Lamb.

And here we are at the final question: Why? What's the point of all this? Again, the answer is the same: *worship*. But this time, with the full drama of redemption unfolded, we find our way *in* to this scene of worship. We get to be part of it. Forever. Falling down and worshiping the Lamb. Only because of the Lamb. The focus of this worship is the redemption of God's people from every tribe and language and people and nation, as God creates from all the corners of the earth a new people for himself, making them (according to v. 10) *a kingdom and priests to our God*, just as he promised Moses back in Exodus 19. Right after God pictured himself in Exodus 19:4 as bearing his people on eagles' wings (how beautiful to see God pictured as an eagle from the beginning to the end . . . carrying us swiftly and safely all the way!), he then promised in Exodus 19:5–6 that if his people would keep his covenant, they would be his treasured possession, *a kingdom of priests and a holy nation.* Well, that was at the beginning of the story, and here we are at the end—and he's done it. His people could not keep his covenant, but Jesus came, and Jesus did, the worthy Lamb of God in our place. Only because this Lamb was slain can we now join the amazing swell of voices in these final sections, with not only the four living creatures and the twenty-four elders but a whole heaven-full of angels, myriads of myriads and thousands of thousands ringing loud—"with a loud voice," Revelation 5:12 tells us.

In one of our conference sessions, a remarkable story was told by Dr. Miyon Chung, associate professor of theology at Torch Trinity Graduate University in Seoul, South Korea.[2] Dr. Chung was talking about another conference, a global conference for women hosted by Torch Trinity and attended by women from 110 different countries, some in which Christians suffer intense persecution. At one point in that conference, a certain group of women from the Middle East broke out praising God: they started singing and just didn't stop. Dr. Chung described how someone went to this group and asked them why they kept on singing, even missing lunch to do so. Their response: "In our country we never get to sing this loud in public." Think how loud most of us can sing in our worship services, if we please. But think how loud it's going to get as the whole universe joins in.

It's not just myriads of angels in this picture. Look at verse 13 to see who joins in: "every creature in heaven and on

---

[2] The TGC conference session ("Stories from Asia: A Call to Celebrate, Learn, and Pray") was an interview with Dr. Chung, conducted by Mindy Belz, editor of *World* magazine. http://thegospel coalition.org/videos/45450617.

earth and under the earth and in the sea, and all that is in them." A universe-wide song grows here, anticipating the very end of the story, as the words of praise pile up like precious stones: power and wealth and wisdom and might and honor and glory and blessing—seven of them, actually, in that one phrase—and all of them together reflecting and praising the Lamb of God on the throne of heaven. This ultimate scene of worship is the *why* for which you and I were created, for which everything was created. Worship appropriately has the last word in chapter 5.

Worship should have the last word in our lives. This is what we were created for; this is what we need to be *after* as God's redeemed people, day by day, persevering in faith, offering up our prayers that actually connect live with this scene as those bowls of incense spread their fragrance over it all. This worship of the Lamb is happening right now at the heart of the universe, right there just across the threshold and spreading throughout the universe as people from all directions are joining in. We don't make worship happen; we either join it or we don't—and that means we will either weep with despair or sing with joy.

So let's join and invite others to join and see the worship growing and growing—this worship that is all about that throne in heaven, our creator-redeemer God who reigns, our Lamb who died for us. Carry these pictures of these realities with you, and they will begin to form the template for your life from day to day. They will shape your life more and more into a life of worship until that day comes when we will reign on the earth. And it will be a new heaven and a new earth. But that's for the final chapter.

REFLECTION AND DISCUSSION QUESTIONS

1) What themes and details of Revelation 4–5 have we seen in the previous passages studied (Exodus 19; 1 Kings 8; Isaiah 6; Psalm 40; Matthew 17:1–15; and 2 Corinthians 12)?

2) Apocalyptic literature works through symbolic word pictures. Choose several pictures from these chapters, ones that stand out to you, and think on them. Then write down what these pictures show you about God.

3) Revelation 4–5 shows us scenes of heavenly *worship*. How might taking in these scenes affect our worship, both individually and in the gathering of God's people? How might *forgetting* about these scenes affect our worship?

4) The Bible is all about Jesus, from beginning to end. In what ways do these chapters help us see the glory of who Jesus is?

5) How should Revelation 4–5 affect our thoughts and prayers about the nations of the world?

8

Home at Last

THE SPECTACULAR GOD AT THE CENTER

Revelation 21–22

D. A. CARSON

I'd like to begin with three prefatory remarks. First, this chapter is bound to be a kind of review along at least two axes. First, there is the axis of biblical theology. At Trinity Evangelical Divinity School, those of us who teach first-year students an introductory course in biblical theology sometimes require from our students an essay that explains all the ways that Revelation 21–22 pick up themes from elsewhere in the Bible. The book of Revelation rarely quotes the Old Testament, but almost every verse alludes to it and nowhere more abundantly than in Revelation 21–22. The biblical allusions are so rich and intricate that they almost trip over themselves. These chapters serve as a kind of review of the whole Bible. But these chapters provide a review in another sense: inevitably, I will allude to many things that others have already introduced in earlier chapters of this book. When we survey some of the great texts that tell us how God disclosed himself in spectacular theophanies in the past, we quickly discover that these ideas and revelations culminate here. Do you want to hear the Bible's final word about the holiness of God or the temple or the Lamb or the throne? It is all here. Those trajectories culminate here.

Second, the symbolism that goes into apocalyptic writing (which Kathleen so adroitly described in the last chapter) needs to be viewed on several axes. It is strange to us at first. A friend of mine some years ago was giving out copies of the New Testament to undergraduates on the campus of a British university. He was just passing them out, preparing to evangelize. One particular student received a copy and promised to read it. Some months later my friend came across the chap to whom he had given the New Testament. The chap asked the student if he had enjoyed the book. The student replied, "Well, in fact, I did. It was a bit repetitious at the front end; it sort of tells the same story several times. But I sure like that science fiction at the end." Of course, the book of Revelation is not science fiction, but the student was struggling to find a literary genre he could relate to.

I have an older sister who for some years (four decades ago) served as a missionary in Papua New Guinea. She worked in a tribe that was pre–Stone Age in its technology; that is, the tribals did not even use stones for arrowheads or spearheads, but hardwood like teak on bamboo shafts. Technologically, the tribe was very primitive. Suppose someone from that tribe came out and enabled you, a linguist, to learn their language very well. You worked with that tribal person for five years and became fluent in their language. Then suppose you had the responsibility of going into that tribe (dropped in by helicopter) and explaining to them, using only words (i.e., without any objects to show them) in their language what electricity is. How would you go about it?

I have come here to talk to you about—well, there's no word for it in your language, so we'll coin a new one: call it "electricity." Electricity is like a powerful spirit that runs through hard things like vines. These hard things don't grow, however. They are things we make in very, very big mud huts that we call factories. We loop them from tree to tree. (Actually, we cut down the trees, cut all the branches off, put the tree back in the ground—never mind. We just loop them from tree to tree.)

This electricity we pump into one end of these hard things like vines, and these hard things like vines then come through our roofs and into square-ish things, where the electricity goes round and round lickety-split (however you say "lickety-split" in this neo-Melanesian language). It goes around so fast that it makes things hot, and you can actually boil your water in your clay pots without having smoke in your hut. You would no longer need to have a hole in the center of your roof to let out smoke, because there would be no need for fire. You can boil your water and cook your food without fire, using "electricity."

And you can put that same electricity in little round things that we put up in our thatched roofs. Once again it goes lickety-split in these little round things that we make in our big mud huts called factories, and these little round things provide you light like a little sun right in your thatched roof. You could stay up late at night. (Why you'd want to stay up at night, I don't know.)

How am I doing at explaining electricity? I haven't mentioned anything about the atomic or subatomic nature of the physical universe. I haven't talked at all about AC and DC or resistance. I haven't talked about units of measure such as watts and volts and ohms. I haven't talked about power generation or storage. I certainly haven't got into the digital world and talked about semi-resistors and transistors, miniaturized and multiplied to form chips. I haven't explained the rudiments of Boolean algebra, without which there would be no such thing as software code. What's the matter with these people? Are they stupid?

No, of course not. They are no more stupid than we are. The problem is that they have no categories for latching onto these things. They have never seen any of this technology. By contrast, our children grow up with computers and switches and wires and power generation. These things constitute part of their environment. The tribals in my sister's world forty years ago experienced none of these realities, so inevitably your verbal expressions to teach them what electricity is and what it does are full of metaphors and similes: electricity is *like* a spirit that runs along hard things *like* vines, and so forth.

So how will we talk about the throne room of God?

One reason that Scripture uses so much symbolism in its disclosures of God is that we are so dead to God, so blind, so unable to understand, so without categories, so without vocabulary, that when someone like Paul is caught up into the third heaven, the things he sees he is not allowed to describe, but in addition these things are also properly inexpressible because we haven't been there. The biblical writers are forced to resort to institutional and apocalyptic symbolism. The new heaven and the new earth are so far beyond our ken that they are described in categories already disclosed: temple, holy city, king, garden, and priests. These are the categories that God has chosen to use to open our eyes to begin to understand the glory of what is yet to come.

The pieces are already in place: that's what the entire conference was about. The passage before us brings some of them together.

Third, in the Sermon on the Mount, Jesus taught,

> Do not store up for yourselves treasures on earth, where moths and vermin destroy, and where thieves break in and steal. But store up for yourselves treasures in heaven, where moths and vermin do not destroy, and where thieves do not break in and steal. For where your treasure is, there your heart will be also. (Matt. 6:19–21)[1]

We sometimes misunderstand that final aphorism (v. 21). People frequently take it to mean that followers of Jesus should guard their hearts or they will wrongly focus on purely transient treasures. After all, the Bible elsewhere does say, "Above all else, guard your heart, for everything you do flows from it" (Prov. 4:23). But that is not what Jesus is talking about in the Sermon on the Mount. He does not say, "Guard your heart," but rather, "Choose your treasure." Why? Because what you treasure the most is where your heart will go. Your

---

[1] Unless otherwise indicated, Scripture quotations in this chapter are taken from *The Holy Bible, New International Version*®, NIV®. Copyright © 1973, 1978, 1984, 2011 by Biblica, Inc.™ Used by permission. All rights reserved worldwide.

whole being—your mind, emotions, fixations, time, imagination, fantasizing—will follow your treasure. If we are to
treasure the new heaven and the new earth ("heaven" in the
language of Jesus in the Sermon on the Mount), it is extremely
important for Christians to maintain a high evaluation of our
destiny.

There are many reasons why we do not really treasure
heaven all that much:

1) Even when we take the Bible seriously, heaven can be
   reduced to a creedal point but not something that evokes
   images in our imagination and causes us to say, "Yes, yes,
   even so come, Lord Jesus!"

2) In some cases it's biblical ignorance.

3) In some cases we are seduced by the treasures of this world.

4) In some cases it is because we have subjected ourselves to
   visions of a new heaven and a new earth that are pathetically small. We've all seen those little cartoons with people
   in white nightgowns sitting on puffy white clouds while
   they strum harps and wear funny-looking halos over their
   heads. It is easy to start thinking, "You know, I'm pretty
   broad-minded about music. I don't have anything against
   harps. It's nice to have at least one in a good orchestra.
   I wouldn't mind learning to play someday. But after the
   first billion years or so, it might get a wee bit boring. And
   quite frankly, white nightgowns don't suit my complexion.
   If that's what heaven is about, I'm not sure I want to go
   there." But what you find in Scripture is a plethora of images of life to come. We must not overlook their diversity
   and richness. For example, in the parable of the talents,

the master says, "Well done, good and faithful servant! You have been faithful with a few things [fabulous amounts of money, actually]; I will put you in charge of many things. Come and share your master's happiness!" (Matt. 25:21, 23). In other words, it's going to involve not only happiness but work with greater responsibilities than anything you've undertaken here. Elsewhere we find images of participating in a great heavenly chorus, of rest, of resplendent holiness. The new heaven and the new earth will involve fantastic opportunities for growth and service. Failure to reflect on the richness of the biblical images diminishes our anticipation of what the Bible tells us is coming.

5) We sometimes think that the new heaven and the new earth will mean that we suddenly know everything. But omniscience is not a communicable attribute of God—that is, it is not an attribute of God that he can share with non-God. God has many attributes that we must imitate, but omniscience is not one of them. I cannot see why from Scripture there is any reason to think that we'll suddenly somehow know everything once the new heaven and the new earth have dawned. I think we'll just be on the next stage of learning a great deal. After all, we're told that there will be people there "from every tribe and language and people and nation" (Rev. 5:9). Those distinctions are going to apparently continue in heaven. Residents of the new heaven and the new earth will not all have pale faces like mine. I suspect that all the languages will be there, too. And if it takes me a million years to learn Mandarin, who cares? We'll be growing forever and ever in the diversity and richness of this culminating abode.

So it is time to focus on the passage before us. What do we find in this section of Scripture? We find:

1) What is new (21:1–8)
2) What is symbol-laden about the new Jerusalem (21:9–21)
3) What is missing (21:22–27)
4) What is central (22:1–5)

On some of these pictures, we'll spend considerable time. On others we'll dance through the text rather quickly.

1) WHAT IS NEW (REV. 21:1–8)

What is new is nothing less than a new heaven and a new earth. As soon as John has made that point, he announces something else that is new: a new Jerusalem.

We begin with the new heaven and the new earth. These images come from the Old Testament. In Isaiah 65:17–19, God says,

> See, I will create
>   new heavens and a new earth.
> The former things will not be remembered,
>   nor will they come to mind.
> But be glad and rejoice forever
>   in what I will create,
> for I will create Jerusalem to be a delight
>   and its people a joy.
> I will rejoice over Jerusalem
>   and take delight in my people;
> the sound of weeping and of crying
>   will be heard in it no more.

So here we have a new heaven and a new earth and a newly renovated Jerusalem, announced by a prophet who is writing in the eighth century before Christ.

Elsewhere, the apostle Peter picks up similar terminology:

> But the day of the Lord will come like a thief. The heavens will disappear with a roar; the elements will be destroyed by fire, and the earth and everything done in it will be laid bare. Since everything will be destroyed in this way, what kind of people ought you to be? You ought to live holy and godly lives as you look forward to the day of God and speed its coming. That day will bring about the destruction of the heavens by fire, and the elements will melt in the heat. But in keeping with his promise we are looking forward to a new heaven and a new earth, where righteousness dwells. (2 Pet. 3:10–13)

I am old enough to remember the apocalyptic horror of threatened nuclear exchange. Some of us remember that in the 1950s in school classrooms all across the United States and Canada we were told what to do if there was a nuclear exchange: hide under the desks! I practiced it. In retrospect it is easy to see that this was an unbelievably stupid response. A lot of people were building underground nuclear safety shelters, complete with a year's supply of food, clean water, and so forth. I remember asking my dad if we should do something like that. He put his hand on my shoulder and said, "Don, when Jesus comes, the very elements will melt with fervent heat. Until then, don't worry about it." In other words, the Bible anticipates something far more final than mere nuclear holocaust. There will be such a renovation of everything that language fails to describe it.

Without using exactly the same language, Paul writes something similar:

> I consider that our present sufferings are not worth comparing with the glory that will be revealed in us. For the creation waits in eager expectation for the children of God to be revealed. For the creation was subjected to frustration, not by its own choice, but by the will of the one who subjected it, in hope that the creation itself will be liberated from its bondage to decay and brought into the freedom and glory of the children of God. We know that the whole creation has been groaning as in the pains of childbirth right up to the present time. (Rom. 8:18–22)

This vision is not some mere ratcheting up of the old universe to some new level of improvement. This is massive renovation, massive transformation. Exactly what this entails is doubtless beyond our capacity to imagine. Exactly what the relationship is between the new heaven and the new earth and the old heaven and the old earth I can scarcely articulate. Yet John provides hints in the passage before us, and they are all spectacular.

"There was no longer any sea" (Rev. 21:1). This is symbol-laden language. These two chapters, Revelation 21–22, are loaded with symbolism. I have not forgotten that in my outline I insist that there is specially focused symbolism in the next section (21:9–21), but that special focus does not diminish the impact of the symbolism throughout these two chapters—and that is true of the use of "sea" in the first verse. I was born and reared in French Canada, but my parents were both born in the United Kingdom, an island nation. So I was brought up reading literature with an island mythology:

I must go down to the seas again, to the lonely sea
  and the sky,
And all I ask is a tall ship and a star to steer her by.
  (John Masefield)

In such a culture, the sea represents adventure, empire, and triumph. But not in the Old Testament:

But the wicked are like the tossing sea,
  which cannot rest,
  whose waves cast up mire and mud. (Isa. 57:20)

What do we read here in Revelation 21:1? "I saw 'a new heaven and a new earth' . . . *and there was no longer any sea.*" If the sea represents muck and chaos, to declare there is no more sea is to announce the abolition of moral dirt. Verse 1 is not talking about the hydrological details of resurrection existence. It is a symbol-laden description of the absolute, utter, complete, abolition of chaos, evil, and mud, in all of its moral dimensions. That is what the new heaven and the new earth will be like.

"I saw the Holy City, the new Jerusalem" (v. 2). This plays on expectations worked out in the Old Testament. One cannot help but remember that Jerusalem was not just another city: it is "the city of the Great King" (Ps. 48:2; Matt. 5:35), of the Davidic dynasty that God himself had established. Equally it is the city of the temple. So it is the city where God rules and where he has provided temple ritual that addresses human sin and enmity. This is Jerusalem. The New Testament picks up on the importance of Jerusalem long before we reach these two closing chapters. In what is perhaps the first letter of the New Testament to be written, Galatians insists that those bound to the old covenant are tied "to the present city of Jerusalem, because she is in slavery with her children"; by contrast, the apostle tells the Galatian believers that "the Jerusalem that is above is free, and she is our mother" (Gal. 4:25–26). Hebrews 12:22 tells us that Christians have already "come to Mount Zion, to the city of the living God, the heavenly Jerusalem."

Moreover, the picture of a city ensures that the final state of bliss is a profoundly *social* vision. A city means lots of people. Some years ago, I was lecturing in Korea, and there were some students attending the school who were from India. On one occasion I was having a meal with them, and one Indian found out that I was from Canada. He asked, "How many citizens are there in Canada?"

At the time I replied, "Something like 28 million."

"And Canada is big?" he asked.

"Yes, the land mass is considerably larger than the continental United States."

"You poor man," he replied.

I said, "I beg your pardon."

"In my state, which is a very small state, we have 147 million. That's wonderful. You have only 28 million, and you're so big. You poor man."

Talk about a culture clash. There are countless people in the Western world who when they think of retirement think of going out in the country, getting away, perhaps a little cottage by a lake, with no near neighbors; peace and quiet; fishing; maybe five or ten miles to the nearest village where you can buy something. Maybe your cell phone doesn't work (blessed release). Oh, sure, increasingly there's a new generation coming along that likes to be urban, but there continues to be a lot of strength in this older mythology of living out in the wild and being away from people.

But that's not the mythology of India.

In the New Testament, cities become symbols that point in different directions. Those of us who have come from rural stock or suburban areas are inclined to think of cities as cesspools of iniquity. But in reality, cities just have more people. Where you have more people you have more sinners—and more righteous people, too. That is why in the book of Revelation there are *two* cities. Babylon represents all that is evil, and the new Jerusalem represents all that is good. Similarly, in the book of Revelation there are two women. Somebody has called this book, "A Tale of Two Cities: The Harlot and the Bride." You come across the evil woman in chapter 17, and she represents all that is wretched. And now we see a city that is simultaneously a bride.

So the vision of the new Jerusalem is a social vision, a city vision, where people come together. And it is David's city, the city of the great king. It is the city with the temple of God. And now the symbolist strikes out in spectacularly fresh ways.

John likens the city to a bride, "coming down out of heaven from God, prepared as a bride beautifully dressed for her husband" (21:2). This element becomes much more intense later in the passage. For the moment he focuses on the city as the dwelling place for God's people, among whom he will dwell: "They will be his people, and God himself will be with them and be their God" (v. 3).

That language is drawn from numerous passages in the Old Testament. Here's Leviticus 26, which in context deals with God's dwelling with his people in the framework of the tabernacle:

> I will put my dwelling place among you, and I will not abhor you. I will walk among you and be your God, and you will be my people. I am the LORD your God, who brought you out of Egypt [there's the exodus] so that you would no longer be slaves to the Egyptians; I broke the bars of your yoke and enabled you to walk with heads held high. (vv. 11–13)

And Jeremiah, six centuries before Christ, promised a new covenant:

> I will put my law in their minds
>   and write it on their hearts.
> I will be their God,
>   and they will be my people. (Jer. 31:33)

In other words, Jeremiah uses language similar to that of Moses but ratcheted up in terms of the new covenant. Ezekiel (also sixth century) writes, "My dwelling place will be with them; I will be their God, and they will be my people" (Ezek. 37:27).

So also here in Revelation:

> And I heard a loud voice from the throne saying, "Look! God's dwelling place is now among the people, and he will dwell with them. They will be his people, and God himself will be with them and be their God. (Rev. 21:3)

Although the same language is used, this passage in its context depicts more than what Moses, Jeremiah, and Ezekiel do. Although the terminology is the same, Revelation

21 depicts what those older passages merely point to. Under the old covenant, God manifested himself in the context of the tabernacle and then the temple; in the prophecies of Jeremiah and Ezekiel, God promises to disclose himself in the context of the new covenant. Now in the consummation, these strands come together in their ultimate fulfillment: God, our God, so makes his dwelling with his people in unshielded glory, such that the blessings of his presence are unqualified, unbounded, unlimited. Everything has been brought to a climax.

What does this mean? What does this look like? The text tells us: "He will wipe every tear from their eyes. There will be no more death or mourning or crying or pain, for the old order of things has passed away" (v. 4). That's not the way it is right now, but when this new Jerusalem comes, the transformation will be so complete that death itself will die. No more tears, no more mourning: this is the *new* heaven and the *new* earth; the *old* order is gone—the order that sin has cursed and that has attracted the wrath of God, the older order in which death has stamped everything and things decay. Despite all the mediating grace of God our world still enjoys (the grace we sometimes call "common grace" because God dispenses it commonly, with the result that many kinds of lovely and beautiful things are still here), the creation is still under the curse. But now in Revelation 21, the old order is gone.

I can't imagine the dimensions of grief and tears found among all who read these lines. But then there will be no more tears. There will be no more death. There will be no more mourning. For the old order of things will have passed away.

In this passage, of course, eternal blessedness is still couched in negation: the new heaven and the new earth will *not* be like the old one that is passing away. We are given a glimpse into what will *no longer* be there: death and sorrow and decay. We still have not yet seen what *will be* there. There are hints, of course, bound up with the opposite of the bad things that come to an end. If tears dry up, there must be joy; if death dies, there must be life. This kind of polarity derives from many Old Testament passages:

> And those the LORD has rescued will return.
> They will enter Zion with singing;
>   everlasting joy will crown their heads.
> Gladness and joy will overtake them,
>   and sorrow and sighing will flee away. (Isa. 35:10)

Or a little earlier in the book of Revelation, we read words anticipating this climactic vision:

> Never again will they hunger;
>   never again will they thirst.
> The sun will not beat down on them,
>   nor any scorching heat.
> For the Lamb at the center of the throne
>   will be their shepherd;
> he will lead them to springs of living water.
>   And God will wipe away every tear from their eyes.
>   (Rev. 7:16–17)

God "will swallow up death forever" (Isa. 25:8).

Suddenly your mind goes to other parts of the Bible that anticipate the end, for example, the great resurrection chapter

(1 Corinthians 15). We will have bodies like Christ's resurrection body. The best analogy Paul can think of to explain the relationship between our current body and the resurrection body to come is the relationship between an acorn and a tree. They are somehow tied but so spectacularly different. Paul says that this resurrection body is a "spiritual body," but the New Testament depicts it as a body that can be touched and handled, a body that eats. We will have spiritual bodies like Christ's resurrection body and so, to that degree, physical as well. Our destiny is not some *mere* heaven, understood as some sort of ethereal existence. Our hope is a new heaven *and a new earth*, a social existence in the new Jerusalem.

In Revelation 21:5, for the first time in this chapter, God speaks. The language is weighty. It's as if every significant clause must be separately introduced to give you time to stop and think about it.

> He who was seated on the throne said, "I am making everything new!" [pause] Then he said, "Write this down, for these words are trustworthy and true." [pause] He said to me: "It is done." (vv. 5–6a)

Unlike revelations that have been sealed up for a later time, this one is written down for us to read. We recall that the Savior on the cross cried, "It is finished" (John 19:30). Here the voice on the throne cries, "It is done."

When Christ cried out, "It is finished," he was saying that all the needed sacrifice had been accomplished. There was no more payment for sin needed, for all the sins of the past and that would take place in the future had been covered. God's holiness was utterly and completely satisfied. It is finished.

But that does not mean that there is no more struggle. As Revelation 12 points out, precisely because Satan knows that he is defeated, "he is filled with fury, because he knows that his time is short" (v. 12). And that is why "our struggle is not against flesh and blood, but against the rulers, against the authorities, against the powers of this dark world and against the spiritual forces of evil in the heavenly realms" (Eph. 6:12).

But now it is done: the entire struggle is over. All the gospel promises that we have enjoyed in some measure in our life here, in powerful reality but still only in anticipation, now come to consummation. The voice from the throne says to write this: "It is done."

The voice who is speaking like this discloses himself: "I am the Alpha and the Omega, the Beginning and the End" (Rev. 21:6). He is the only one who could bring it all to pass. He was there at the beginning; he is present at the end. The Alpha and the Omega has brought everything he promised to pass. And it is done.

When John reports these words from God, they are addressed to people who know that the consummation is not here yet, however impending it may be. So they hear the gracious invitation of this God: "To the thirsty I will give water without cost from the spring of the water of life" (v. 6). Once again, this language is drawn from the Old Testament:

> Come, all you who are thirsty,
>   come to the waters;
> and you who have no money,
>   come, buy and eat!
> Come, buy wine and milk
>   without money and without cost. (Isa. 55:1)

It is without cost to those who receive it, but it is not without cost to him who provided it.

Revelation 21:7 is badly translated in the translation from which I am reading (NIV): "Those who are victorious will inherit all this, and I will be their God and they will be my children." In the original, verse 7 is written in the singular and mentions a son, and in this context those details need to be preserved: "The one who is victorious [who is a conqueror] will inherit all this, and I will be his God and he will be my son." Of course, the people who will inherit all this, and who will be called God's "son," include both men and women. That's what the NIV is trying to preserve. In this instance, however, the word "son" is so much bound up with a symbolism that runs right through Scripture that you've just got to preserve the word. Let me explain.

In our culture, the overwhelming majority of sons do not end up doing what their fathers have done vocationally; the overwhelming majority of daughters do not end up doing what their mothers have done vocationally. Under 5 percent of contemporaries end up actually doing vocationally what their parents did at the same age. But in the ancient world it was not like that. If you were a boy in the ancient world, if your father was a farmer, you became a farmer. If your father was a baker, you became a baker. It was part of the heritage. Thus, your identity was bound up with your father's name and job (if you were a boy).

Out of this social reality comes an array of biblical metaphors. Several people are called "sons of Belial" or "sons of worthlessness." If you are called a "son of worthlessness," it does not mean that you must be male, or that your physical father or mother is worthless; rather, it means that your character is so disgustingly worthless that the only explanation is that you belong to the Worthless family.

Again, when in the Beatitudes Jesus says, "Blessed are the peacemakers, for they will be called the sons [NIV children] of God" (ESV), he is not trying to eliminate women. He is picking up a similar metaphorical use of "son": God is the supreme peacemaker, and insofar as we make peace, we are acting like God and thus show ourselves to be a son of God and thus to belong to the God family. Jesus is not saying that you become a Christian by making peace; he is declaring that peacemaking is so Godlike that if you make peace, then, at least on that axis, you show yourself to be a son of God.

Again, this is why Scripture holds up Abraham as the father of the faithful. Abraham believed in God, and those who believe as Abraham believed are called the sons of Abraham, the children of Abraham: they belong to Abraham's family.

This helps us understand Jesus's argument in John 8 when he finds himself in dispute with some Jewish people who were arguing with him. They claimed to be children of Abraham, and he said that that could not be since Abraham recognizes him while they do not. He is not denying the genetics, as if he were denying their physical descent from Abraham; he is pushing at something deeper. They don't get it; in fact, they up the ante and say, "In fact, we're sons of God." "Oh, no, you're not," Jesus replies, "I know God. God knows me. If you don't recognize me, you can't possibly be sons of God. Let me tell you who your daddy is. You are of your father the Devil. He was a liar from the beginning, and you are telling lies. He was a murderer from the beginning, and you are trying to kill me. Your father is the Devil himself." The issue, once again, is *conduct*.

If a boy were reared in a farmer's family, then his dad taught him to farm, where to plant, when to plant, how to dig ditches, how to sink fence posts—he gave his son his identity. That's why Jesus in the days of his flesh is sometimes called "the carpenter's son"—he is identified with his perceived father Joseph—and then apparently after Joseph has died, in one remarkable passage, Jesus himself is called "the carpenter" (Mark 6:3). Apparently he had taken over the family business. That's his public identity at that juncture.

So "son of God" language is remarkable. The Old Testament calls Israel God's son. "Let my son go, so he may worship me" (Ex. 4:23). Individual believers are sometimes called God's sons. The king of Israel is called God's son, for when he embarks on his role as king, he enters into this sonship because in this respect he is supposed to be acting like God; God is the supreme ruler, and the king now rules in the name of God, in the place of God, reflecting God. He is God's son. In the New Testament it is not uncommon for Christians to be called the sons of God or the children of God, even though they sometimes display decidedly ungodly characteristics.

But now there are no caveats, no footnotes, no sidebars. Revelation 21:7 reads, literally, "The one who is victorious will inherit all this, and *I will be his God and he will be my son*."

What that means is that we who are Christians (whether we are men or women) will at that point perfectly reflect God. After all, we were originally made in his image; and if the image has been horribly distorted and soiled, now we are coming into a fullness and a perfection that is without flaw or inconsistency. We will reflect God. We will be like him in every way that humans can be like him. Of course, there are some ways in which we will *never* be like God. The Bible says, "Be holy, because I am holy" (Lev. 11:44; 1 Pet. 1:16); it does not say, "Be omnipotent, because I am omnipotent." So there are some ways in which we cannot be like God and must not try to be like God. But in any way we should be like God, we will be like God: "I will be his God and he will be my son."

Oh, of course, according to the apostle Paul, you and I *are* sons of God already by adoption. We are his sons *now*. But God help us, there is so much inconsistency, so much sin, so much tension remaining in our lives. One day, all that tension will be gone. There will be no more sin, death, sorrow, two-facedness, and hypocrisy. Do you realize that for all eternity we will never ever have to ask for forgiveness again? Not of each other, not of God himself. For we will be his sons.

The contrast introduced by the next verse, therefore, is painfully, desperately sharp:

> But the cowardly, the unbelieving, the vile, the murderers, the sexually immoral, those who practice magic arts, the idolaters and all liars—they will be consigned to the fiery lake of burning sulfur. This is the second death. (Rev. 21:8)

Revelation previously mentions "the second death" several times (2:11; 20:6, 14). This destruction of fire befalls the Devil and his cohorts: "And the devil, who deceived them, was thrown into the lake of burning sulfur, where the beast and the false prophet had been thrown. They will be tormented day and night for ever and ever" (20:10).

So we will either be the son or the cowardly and the unbelieving.

As far as I can see in Scripture, there is no hint anywhere that people in hell genuinely repent. Even in the parable of the rich man and Lazarus (Luke 16:19–31), the rich man lifts his eyes and somehow is able to see Abraham and Lazarus far off. Considering how he had treated Lazarus while on earth, what do you think the rich man in hell should say? What do you think he would say? "Oh, Lazarus, did I get that one wrong! I am so sorry. Would you please forgive me?" But the rich man does not even address Lazarus. Lazarus was a nobody on earth, and the rich man does not deal with nobodies. He goes to the top. "Father Abraham," he says, "have pity on me and send Lazarus to dip the tip of his finger in water and cool my tongue, because I am in agony in this fire" (v. 24). Where is the repentance? He still thinks he is at the center of the universe; he is still ordering Lazarus around. There is no brokenness, no contrition, no shame. And before the story ends, he is actually arguing theologically with Abraham, correcting Abraham's theology: "No, Father Abraham, you got that one wrong. If someone rose from the dead, then that would really make a difference. Don't you see?" (see v. 30).

Hell is not filled with people who are sorry for their sins. It is filled with people who for all eternity still shake their puny fists in the face of God Almighty in an endless existence of evil and corruption and shame and punishment and the wrath of God.

You sometimes hear people saying stupid things like this: "I want to go to hell because all my friends will be there." There are no friends in hell because when we sinners get together for very long, there is an endless display of one-upmanship, backbiting, sniping, jealousy, hatred, and malice.

So who doesn't get into the new Jerusalem? "The cowardly, the unbelieving, the vile, the murderers, the sexually immoral, those who practice magic arts, the idolaters and all liars." They defy God. The separation is absolute and eternal.

In this text, the very sharpness of the polarity makes the glory of the new heaven and the new earth all the more eminently, superlatively attractive. For there, there is no more sin, sorrow, or mourning.

2) WHAT IS SYMBOL-LADEN ABOUT THE NEW JERUSALEM (REV. 21:9–21)

At one level, of course, there is symbolism everywhere in these chapters. But in what follows, the interpreting angel in the vision goes to great lengths to make John reflect on particular elements of the symbolism related to the new Jerusalem:

> One of the seven angels who had the seven bowls full of the seven last plagues [going back to chap. 16] came and said to me, "Come, I will show you the bride, the wife of the Lamb." And he carried me away in the Spirit to a mountain great and high, and showed me the Holy City, Jerusalem, coming down out of heaven from God. (vv. 9–10)

Just as in chapter 5 the lion is the Lamb (there are not two animals parked side by side), so in chapter 21 the bride is the city. At the beginning of chapter 21, the new Jerusalem comes "down out of heaven from God, prepared as a bride beautifully dressed for her husband" (v. 2). And verses 9–10 identify this bride. The interpreting angel says, in effect, "I am going to show you the bride. She is a city."

For those of you who are not yet married, I earnestly hope that on your wedding day after you have come down the aisle and taken the arm of your groom, he doesn't turn to you sweetly and say, "You are so gorgeous. You look like a city." But apocalyptic can get away with that because it mixes its metaphors. Apocalyptic symbolism provides more than pictures. It provides word pictures that do not have to cohere on the same canvas.

Some cathedrals in Europe have pictures on stained-glass windows of Jesus looking like a lion with a sword coming out of his mouth with part of his body looking like a lamb. Frankly, they look stupid, partly because they present Jesus as part lamb and part lion, not quite one or the other. And he has a sword sticking out of his mouth. Why doesn't he spit it out, for goodness' sake? These are not ordinary pictures; they are word pictures that you're not supposed to paint, precisely because word pictures can allow mixed metaphors. The lion *is* the Lamb.

That is one reason that preaching is so important. You cannot paint a compelling mural of much of the symbolism in the Apocalypse. You end up with something that is frankly laughable. But the word pictures themselves are powerful. The lion is the Lamb, and the bride is the city. We must bring all the different components together in our mind at the same time.

The bride, we are told, is "beautifully dressed for her husband" (v. 2); we anticipate the wedding supper of the Lamb, already mentioned in Revelation 19:9. That brings together a massive typology that runs right through Scripture. In the Old Testament Yahweh himself is the groom, and Israel is the bride. In the New Testament Christ is the groom, and the church is the bride. Out of this evocative metaphorical structure spring many other metaphors. That is why, for example, the Old Testament, from Deuteronomy on, regularly depicts apostasy as a kind of spiritual adultery. Some of the language the Old Testament uses to get that across is frighteningly grotesque to make sure that we get the point: read, for example, Ezekiel 16 and 23. Pray your way through Hosea. This is why Paul can say to the church in Corinth, "I promised you to one husband, to Christ, so that I might present you as a pure virgin to him" (2 Cor. 11:2). And now we have the marriage of the Lamb, to use the language of Revelation 21:2; there is a further metaphorical extension. One can easily grasp what is meant by an expression such as "the wife of the Messiah," but "the wife of the Lamb" (v. 9)? This is an image upon an image. Are we talking about lambs having weddings? But this lamb is the slaughtered Lamb that is also the lion that is getting married to the bride, who is also the church, which is also the city. You must absorb all of these components and start pondering your way through the individual elements.

What's bound up with this bride language? One of the intriguing things that Jesus taught is that there is no marriage in heaven. For those of you who are in really good marriages, you must have wondered once in a while, "I'm sure going to miss it. A renovated universe without marriage doesn't seem like a very good idea." But as far as I can make out, the intimacies and joys (including even sexual intimacies and joys) enthused over and enjoyed in a good marriage are merely a tiny picture of the rapture of intimacy to be enjoyed between Christ and his church.

For you who are single, I know singleness can be hard. But if you are Christ's, fifty billion years from now it will never enter your mind to say, "I was wronged, for I was never permitted to enjoy marriage." But the intimacy you will enjoy in the new heaven and the new earth as part of the church, which is the bride of Christ—we do not even have the language to describe it. It will be such overwhelming, joyful intimacy that the best, most ecstatic marriage pales in comparison.

At the same time, the bride is also a city. What do we learn about this city, the new Jerusalem coming down out of heaven?

"It shone with the glory of God" (v. 11). God is supremely manifesting himself. This is the perfection of God's manifestation. This is the epitome of all of that God has promised, the culmination of all the self-manifestations of God that have been the focus of this series of addresses.

"Its brilliance was like that of a very precious jewel, like a jasper, clear as crystal" (v. 11). Most of our translations say things like "clear as crystal," but in the first century, crystal wasn't clear. They didn't know how to cut glass on perfect angles, and the glass itself was never perfectly transparent. The Greek suggests, rather, that the new Jerusalem is *sparkling* like crystal. It is not transparent but sparkling, spectacular, wonderful.

Think of Princess Kate's sapphire and diamonds. To try to find a suitable analogy, I sometimes mention the Crown Jewels. Have you ever been to London and seen the Crown

Jewels? There are two paths among the cases displaying the Crown Jewels in the Tower of London. There is an inside path adjacent to the cases where all of these spectacular jeweled swords and crowns and individual items are displayed with light shining down on them. If you are on that inside path, close to the glass, there are signs that tell you to keep moving. The guards tell you not to stop. Alternatively, if you are a yard and a half back on the second path, you are allowed to stop. You may pause and watch all of the refracted light broken up into endless colorful beams by the jewels spread out before you. Then move your head a centimeter to the left or right and watch the brilliant kaleidoscopic changes. Then toss your head back and forth quickly, and there's brilliance everywhere.

The last time I went, I took the inside path and then stopped so that I could look a little more closely. Those jewels are spectacular! And then the guard says, "Keep moving. Keep moving." Descriptions of the new Jerusalem along such lines as these are akin to what it's like for an animist with pre–Stone Age technology to understand something about electricity.

> It had a great, high wall with twelve gates, and with twelve angels at the gates. On the gates were written the names of the twelve tribes of Israel. There were three gates on the east, three on the north, three on the south and three on the west. The wall of the city had twelve foundations, and on them were the names of the twelve apostles of the Lamb. (vv. 12–14)

Twelve. That number is significant, as we shall see. Even the points on the compass are specified: "east . . . north . . .

south . . . west." That ordering may be significant, too. Some have argued that when the stones are placed around a square in the order given here in verse 13, and then compared with the twelve signs of the zodiac, the order is the *exact opposite* of the path of the sun through the twelve signs. If so, this order-ing may be a subtle insistence that it has nothing to do with pagan speculations about the city of the gods.

And the city is built like a cube, 12,000 stadia per side. Do you realize how big that is? It's about 1,400 miles. That's about the distance from Chicago to California. But if it is built like a cube, it is about 1,400 miles on edge. In Chicago we have spectacular skyscrapers and wonderful architecture, but when I fly into O'Hare and look over the city, it never makes me think of a cube. What is the point of this symbolism?

This city cannot possibly be Jerusalem in the Middle East; its dimensions make that impossible, and its shape shows it not to be a literal city. There is only one cube in the Old Testament. It is the Most Holy Place, the place in the temple where only the high priest could enter and only then once a year, carrying the blood of bullock and goat for his own sins and the sins of the people.

But now the veil has been torn. It is finished. Now the entire city is the holy place. There is no need for a mediating priest in the order of Levi. There is no outer court. There is no court for the Gentiles or court for women or court for foreign tribes. The whole city is the place where God dwells. It is the Most Holy Place. And it is massive. There's room enough for all, shown by the *twelve hundred* stadia on each edge, calling to mind the totality of the people of God.

The number twelve comes up again and again in Revelation. *Twelve* thousand stadia on edge; again, the wall is "144 cubits thick" (v. 17), and of course, 12 x 12 = 144. A regular symbol in apocalyptic literature for all of God's people is twelve: twelve tribes of the Old Testament and twelve apostles of the New Testament.

Incidentally, you must not think that numbers are always symbol-laden in Scripture. Many times they are not. But they are virtually always symbol-laden in apocalyptic literature. Here is the city built like a cube (12,000 stadia per side), the place where the Old Testament and New Testament people of God are brought together.

I wish I had the time to work through these various stones (vv. 18–21). But I'm going to skip to the last two points. They are the most important points of all.

3) WHAT IS MISSING (REV. 21:22–27)

What is missing from this city?

"I did not see a temple in the city, because the Lord God Almighty and the Lamb are its temple" (v. 22). Of course, in one sense you cannot imagine a temple in this city because the city is itself the Most Holy Place. Or to change the metaphor a bit, there is no temple here because there is no mediating structure necessary anymore. We are there in the presence of God.

Repeatedly after chapters 4–5, mention of God in the book of Revelation is coupled with mention of the Lamb or the Messiah. For instance, in Revelation 7:10 we read, "Salvation belongs to our God, who sits on the throne, and to the Lamb" (see also 7:15; 11:15; 12:10; 16:7; 21:22). Here God and the Lamb are brought together one more time (21:22); once more we are transported back to the great vision of Revelation 4–5. This reminds us that all that God has brought about, he has brought about through the gospel, through the Lamb, through the Lamb who is the king, through the Lamb who is the lion, through the Lamb who is the sacrifice, through the Lamb who has brought to pass all the plans of God held in the scroll in the Almighty's right hand. Now the time of mediation is past: there is no Old Testament temple and sacrificial system, and there is not even a separate mediating function assigned to Christ (cf. 1 Cor. 15:25–28); rather, all is complete: "I did not see a temple in the city, because the Lord God Almighty and the Lamb are its temple."

"The city does not need the sun or the moon to shine on it, for the glory of God gives it light, and the Lamb is its lamp" (Rev. 21:23). There is no sea in the new heaven and the new earth (v. 1); now we are told that there is no sun or moon above the holy city. Just as the absence of the sea had nothing to do with the hydrological features of the new heaven and the new earth, so the absence of the sun has nothing to do with mere astronomical features. The point is far more profound. All that we know of light in this world comes from the created order with its cycles and limitation, but in the consummation we find ourselves in the light of God—unqualified light, with no darkness at all, not even any cycles of day and night. Night is often bound up with the works of darkness where people are hiding and skulking. But here there is no night. "For the glory of God gives it light." All that God is gives it light.

"The nations will walk by its light, and the kings of the earth will bring their splendor into it" (v. 24). All the different cultures bring in what has been formed and shaped and given by God's grace, now completely purified and transformed, with spectacular displays of cultural heritage.

"On no day will its gates ever be shut, for there will be no night there" (v. 25). You shut gates at night to stop robbers and thugs from getting in. This place is secure; there is no night.

> The glory and honor of the nations will be brought into it. Nothing impure will ever enter it, nor will anyone who does what is shameful or deceitful, but only those whose names are written in the Lamb's book of life. (vv. 26–27)

4) WHAT IS CENTRAL (REV. 22:1–5)

What is central? There are two things:

4.1) *The Water of Life from the Throne of God and of the Lamb (Rev. 22:1–3)*

> Then the angel showed me the river of the water of life, as clear as crystal, flowing from the throne of God and of the Lamb down the middle of the great street of the city. On each side of the river stood the tree of life [harking back to Genesis], bearing twelve crops of fruit, yielding its fruit every month. And the leaves of the tree are for the healing of the nations. (vv. 1–2)

It almost sounds as if there will still be national structures of some sort. Why not, if there are tribes and peoples and languages? But there will be no sickness, decay, fighting, or war. Everything finally comes from God and the cross. This is an utter transformation. "No longer will there be any curse"

(v. 3). The curse of Genesis 3 is gone; it has been utterly removed, for the cross has done its work (Revelation 4–5).

"The throne of God and of the Lamb will be in the city, and
his servants will serve him" (Rev. 22:3).

But the best part is found in verses 4–5.

4.2) The Beatific Vision (Rev. 22:4–5)

"They will see his face" (v. 4). In the history of the Christian
church this is often called "the Beatific Vision," the vision of
the Blessed One.

Those great seraphic beings described in Isaiah 6 had to
cover their faces and could not look on the face of this God.
Even when you study theophanies that recount someone seeing God in some fashion or another, the surrounding context
always limits it in some way. So, yes, Isaiah "saw the Lord,"
but what he really saw was the temple filled with smoke, and
when he lifted his eyes upward he did not see much more
than the hem of God's garment. Everything above that is not
easily describable. Or think of the vision of God sitting on
his mobile throne-chariot in Ezekiel 1. The description of the
chariot is fairly detailed, but when you get to the description
of the one who sits on it, what Ezekiel sees is "the appearance
of the likeness of the glory of the LORD" (v. 28). You certainly
cannot draw it.

But now? Can you grasp what this text says? God's redeemed people do something that even angels cannot do!
"They will see his face" (Rev. 22:4)! And they will not die.
They will not be ashamed. They will not be consumed. They
will be as much like God as his image bearers can be without
being God. They will be his son.

And the church sings:

Face to face with Christ my Savior.
Face to face, what will it be
When with rapture I behold him,
Jesus Christ who died for me?[2]

I've talked to a lot of Christians who are eager to get to heaven so they can see their long-lost relatives. My mother died of complications from Alzheimer's. On the last day, the Lord Jesus will say, in effect, "Elizabeth Margaret Maybury Carson, arise!" And she will rise in resurrection splendor. But when I read the Apocalypse, I do not find a lot of Christians saying, "I can hardly wait to see my dad and mum again." The culmination of everything is to see God: "They will see his face."

In some measure we "see" God already; by the eyes of faith, in the person of Christ, in the glory and the shame of the cross, and by the gift of the Spirit, we enjoy some wonderful foretastes, seeing, as it were, through a glass darkly. But one day we will see God face-to-face.

Usually when I go somewhere to speak, it's far enough away that I fly. But sometimes it's not too far away, and I drive. On those occasions I listen to talks, sermons, and music. My music tastes are pathetically eclectic. Some time ago I was listening to Roger Whitaker sing folk songs from around the world. He sang of Cape Breton (any Canadian will appreciate that).

If my time could end perfectly,
I know how I'd want it to be;
God's gift of heaven would be made up of three:
My love, Cape Breton, and me.

---

[2] Carrie E. Breck, "Face to Face with Christ My Savior," 1898.

And I thought to myself, "My dear Roger Whitaker, you just defined hell." For Roger Whitaker and his "love" will breed like rabbits and produce new generations of sinners. Pretty soon we will be threatened with nuclear holocaust and again wallow in all the hate and enmity and lust and war and malice that we know already. And Cape Breton itself will be a wasteland under the curse of God.

"God's gift of heaven would be made up of three"? Heaven centers absolutely on the one—the one triune God. We shall see his face, and every joy will be perfected. Every ecstasy will be beyond measure. Every intimacy will be superb. In this new Jerusalem we will sing our hearts out in spectacular choirs; we will work and worship and grow and learn more of God as for all eternity we explore the infinite dimensions of his grace. And even then we will only be scratching the surface. We will see his face.

CONCLUSION

Not surprisingly the book of Revelation ends in spectacular invitation. I am certain that some who read these lines have never trusted Christ Jesus. Do you see how this book ends?

> The Spirit and the bride say, "Come!" And let the one who hears say, "Come!" Let the one who is thirsty come; and let the one who wishes take the free gift of the water of life. (v. 17)

> "He who testifies to these things says, 'Yes, I am coming soon'" (v. 20a). We join Christians of every age across every continent and generation and tribe and say, "Amen. Come, Lord Jesus" (v. 20b).

REFLECTION AND DISCUSSION QUESTIONS

1) Reflect on some of the ways Revelation 21–22 offers a culminating vision of God—one that pulls together all the passages we've studied so far (Exodus 19; 1 Kings 8; Isaiah 6; Psalm 40; Matt. 17:1–15; 2 Corinthians 12; and Revelation 4–5).

2) Don Carson talks about the importance of *treasuring heaven*. What does he mean, what keeps you from treasuring heaven, and what in these chapters encourages you to do so?

3) What about this *city*, this new Jerusalem? What pictures of this city in Revelation 21–22 particularly capture your imagination and why?

4) How does Jesus shine through all these pictures? How do these chapters help you treasure and long to see Jesus?

5) The passages we've studied have been all about seeing God. The Bible's final two chapters picture the culmination of that reality and that hope. Look through Revelation 21–22 one more time, and then write a concluding prayer to this God who so graciously reveals himself to us.

Contributors

PAIGE BROWN

After graduating from the University of Mississippi, Paige Brown completed a master's degree at Covenant Theological Seminary. She served with Reformed University Fellowship at Vanderbilt University and the University of Virginia and as a teacher on staff at Park Cities Presbyterian Church (Dallas). Paige and her husband, Reagan, live in Nashville with their three children.

D. A. CARSON

D. A. Carson (PhD, University of Cambridge) is cofounder and president of The Gospel Coalition and since 1978 has taught at Trinity Evangelical Divinity School (Deerfield, IL), where he currently serves as Research Professor of New Testament. He came to Trinity from Northwest Baptist Theological Seminary in Vancouver, British Columbia, and has served in pastoral ministry in Canada and the United Kingdom. He and his wife, Joy, have two children.

NANCY LEIGH DEMOSS

Through her ministry Revive Our Hearts, Nancy Leigh DeMoss (University of Southern California) calls women to heart revival and biblical womanhood. Her love for the Word and the Lord Jesus permeates her online outreaches, conference messages, numerous books, and nationally syndicated radio programs, *Revive Our Hearts* and *Seeking Him with Nancy Leigh DeMoss.*

TIM KELLER

Tim Keller serves as senior pastor of Redeemer Presbyterian Church in Manhattan, a church he planted in 1989, with his wife, Kathy, and their three sons. Originally from Pennsylvania, he was educated at Bucknell University; Gordon-Conwell Theological Seminary; and Westminster Theological Seminary. He is cofounder and vice president of The Gospel Coalition.

KATHLEEN NIELSON

Kathleen Nielson (PhD, Vanderbilt University) is director of women's initiatives for The Gospel Coalition. She has taught in the English departments at Vanderbilt; Bethel College (MN); and Wheaton College, authored Bible studies, and loves ministering to women in churches and conferences near and far. Kathleen and her husband, Niel, have three sons, two daughters-in-law, and three granddaughters.

JOHN PIPER

John Piper is founder and teacher of DesiringGod.org, chancellor of Bethlehem College and Seminary, and a founding council member of The Gospel Coalition. For thirty-three years he served as senior pastor at Bethlehem Baptist Church (Minneapolis). He studied at Wheaton College; Fuller Theological Seminary (BD); and the University of Munich (DTh). He and his wife, Noël, have four sons, one daughter, and twelve grandchildren.

JENNY SALT

Jenny Salt (MDiv, Trinity Evangelical Divinity School) is dean of students at Sydney Missionary and Bible College, where she has served since 1997. She shares her passion for expository Bible teaching and equipping in women's conferences throughout Australia, South Africa, and New Zealand. She loves enjoying time with family (including six nieces and nephews).

CARRIE SANDOM

Carrie Sandom (BTh, University of Oxford) has served in women's ministry for over twenty years, with students in Cambridge and young professionals in London before moving to St. John's, Tunbridge Wells, where she currently works with women of all ages and stages of life. An experienced conference speaker, Carrie also trains women for Bible teaching ministry at the Cornhill Training Course in London and cohosts the annual Proclamation Trust women in ministry conference.

General Index

Scripture Index